HAPPY QUILTS!

HAPPY QUILTS!

10 FUN, KID-THEMED QUILTS AND COORDINATING SOFT TOYS

ANTONIE ALEXANDER

Fons&Porter
CINCINNATI, OHIO

CONTENTS

INTRODUCTION

I started this journey almost twelve months ago. It began with a simple email, a few lines asking whether I would be interested in writing a book. I can't begin to explain the excitement I felt or how overwhelmed I was by the prospect of it all.

As I write this, I am sitting on the beach listening to the call of seagulls, sipping a wonderfully frothy coffee and wondering what to write as the introduction to this, my first book. How can I possibly convey to you, through words alone, the way the colors and textures of fabric, the endless possibilities it offers, make my heart sing.

I've always loved working with fabric. I don't think my middle school teacher will ever forget the life-sized human doll I made for art class! The joy of creating something both beautiful and useful from scraps of fabric enraptured me, and I've not stopped since.

When my children were born, I started making fun, happy quilts and soft toys for them. I was thrilled to see them dragging their quilts and soft toys around, making blanket forts to play in, snuggling with them when they were sleepy or sick. It never mattered if they got dirty; a quick cycle in the washing machine and they were clean again. My quilts and soft toys are made to be used and, most of all, loved.

I want your children and grandchildren to have as much fun with these quilts and soft toys as mine did, and I want you to have fun making them. Experiment with the designs, take a block from one quilt and pop it in another, make a soft toy for every member of your family or use the individual appliqué blocks for something entirely different.

Just do and make what makes you happiest—this book is called *Happy Quilts* after all!

toni xx

CHAPTER ONE
TOOLS & TECHNIQUES FOR SUCCESSFUL QUILT AND SOFT TOY MAKING

To make the quilts and soft toys in this book, you will need some essential tools and equipment. All the projects in this book are fairly straightforward. They are easy to make and are suitable for confident beginners as well as more experienced sewers. However, I always recommend that novices participate in face-to-face sewing and quilting classes.

If you're not familiar with some of the basic techniques used to make the quilts or soft toys, I've included straightforward tutorials here. I've also included a few tips throughout to make sewing your quilt or soft toy as simple and fun as possible.

ESSENTIAL TOOLS & MATERIALS

Cutting Tools

Patchwork is made much easier by the use of a rotary cutter, ruler and mat. Choose tools you are comfortable with, especially your rotary cutter. My favorite cutting mat is self-healing and measures 24" × 36" (61cm × 91.4cm); it covers three-quarters of my work surface and is big enough to handle most cutting jobs. I prefer to use a 6" × 24" (15.2cm × 61cm) ruler with 45-degree angle lines marked on it.

Remember to change the blade in your rotary cutter regularly for ease of cutting and to avoid snagging your fabric. Always cut away from yourself and keep your fingers out of the way of the cutting blade!

Scissors

Use sharp dressmaker's scissors for cutting fabric and craft scissors for cutting paper patterns and templates. A small pair of sharp embroidery scissors is perfect for cutting in and around small template pieces and for snipping threads.

Needles and Pins

You will require a selection of sewing machine needles, chosen for the type of fabric you are using, and hand-sewing needles for embroidery. I like to use good quality appliqué and embroidery needles with a slightly larger eye for ease of threading. Safety pins are also used to baste the various layers of the quilt sandwich before quilting.

Marking Tools

I use a sharpened lead pencil or a Pigma Micron Permanent Marker pen, usually in blue or brown, to draw the features and details on my quilts and soft toys. There are water- and air-soluble markers, as well as chalk pencils, available that can be used to mark your fabric temporarily. Always test these markers on a scrap of fabric before using them on your project.

BASIC QUILT-MAKING TOOLKIT

Quilter's ruler

Rotary cutter

Cutting mat

Tape measure

Scissors (both fabric and craft)

Pins

Sewing machine

Needles (both sewing machine and hand) and coordinating threads

Pencils and fabric markers

Iron

Fusible webbing

Appliqué mat

Light box (optional)

BASIC SOFT TOY-MAKING TOOLKIT

Scissors (both fabric and craft)

Straight pins

Sewing machine

Needles (both sewing maching and hand) and coordinating threads

Pencils and fabric markers

Polyester fiberfill

Wooden dowel or chopstick (to aid stuffing)

Fusible webbing

Light Box

A light box is a very useful piece of equipment for tracing and reversing templates. You can use a well-lit window if you don't have access to a light box. To trace onto fabric, use tape to secure the template to the light box or window, then tape the fabric on top. Carefully trace the markings onto the fabric using a sharp, light lead pencil or fabric marker.

Thread

My choice for machine piecing quilts is cotton thread with a polyester core. This combination gives a smooth, snag-free finish and is durable and strong. Many quilters prefer to use 100% cotton thread, and I leave this decision to you.

You should always use a good quality polyester sewing thread when you are sewing soft toys to ensure strong, durable seams. Polyester thread does not snag or break easily, and it has a slight give, making it ideal for stitching fabrics with a slight stretch.

In addition to thread, I also use six-stranded DMC embroidery floss for stitching around my appliqué pieces and for stitching details such as faces on the soft toys and quilts.

A multitude of different thread types are available, including specialty threads such as metallics and glow-in-the-dark thread. Have fun experimenting!

Buttons

I like to use buttons on my quilts and soft toys. They are readily available and simple to sew on, and you can find them in myriad colors, sizes and shapes. Unfortunately, buttons can present a choking hazard and thus are not suitable for children under three years of age. If you are making a toy or quilt for a young child, use appliqué or embroidery to replace the buttons. Child-safe doll eyes are another option.

Child-safe doll eyes are available at most large craft stores or online. The eyes come in many colors, sizes and shapes. They have a long plastic prong on the back that pokes through the fabric and a washer that secures them in place. They are recommended if your soft toy is for a child under three years of age. Always check the product details for suitability.

Toy Filling

Polyester toy filling or polyester fiberfil is recommended for its nonallergenic qualities and its washing and drying ease. You can readily find polyester fiberfil in any good craft store. Buy good quality fiberfil that has lots of bounce to it. Use a wooden dowel or a wooden chopstick to push the stuffing into place.

If you would like to add weight to your soft toy, perhaps in the bottom or the legs, you may want to stuff those areas with polypropylene pellets. Experiment with a combination of polyester toy filling and pellets to get the desired effect. Remember that poly beads aren't suitable for young children under three years of age as they are a choking hazard if they spill from the soft toy.

CHOKING HAZARD

Buttons present a choking hazard for children under three years of age. If making a quilt or soft toy for a young child, replace the buttons with appliqué, embroidery or child-safe doll eyes when appropriate.

Fabric

Most quilters prefer working with 100% cotton fabric, but it can be great fun to experiment with other types of fabric. Try using flannel or velour, for example, when appliquéing animals like teddy bears. These fabrics add a fantastic soft texture to the animals that makes them stand out from the rest of the quilt.

Always adapt your sewing techniques to suit the fabrics you are using; make a test block first to see if your fabric choices work well together. Some heavier fabrics might create bulky seams; simply press these seams open to distribute the bulk. Most of all, have fun, experiment, learn from your mistakes and make gorgeous quilts. Remember, it's your quilt and you get to make the decisions!

Don't be afraid of color and pattern. Take a deep breath and trust yourself. Trust your instincts: if a piece of fabric looks wrong, it probably is. When fabric shopping, pull out bolts of fabric or precuts and place them next to each other. Look at how they work together: your instinct will tell you if something's wrong. Screw up your eyes and squint at the fabric, or take a photograph and look at it on the screen; it really helps!

Pure white fabric can appear harsh against softer colors. Try using an off-white or soft, light cream-colored fabric instead. Black can also appear very harsh; try substituting dark charcoal or the darkest brown-colored fabric to soften the contrast.

Many of my quilts are sewn using scraps and fabrics from my stash. It's fun and exciting to consider all the wonderful possibilities fabrics have to offer. Working with many different fabrics adds interest to your quilt. Select fabrics that contrast in color and pattern: polka dots, checks, stripes and floral prints add visual interest. Don't be afraid to join smaller pieces of fabric together to make larger pieces.

The soft toys can be made from almost any fabric: cotton, felt, corduroy, velvet, fleece, denim and faux fur just to name a few. Try out a wide variety of fabrics, including recycled clothing, to make a soft toy that's unique to you. Combine two or even three different types of fabric to create textural and visual interest. Don't be afraid to experiment! Corduroy, velvet and fleece are beautiful to work with and feel wonderfully cuddly and soft; cotton fabric is readily available and comes in an enormous range of colors and patterns. Your choices are endless, so jump in feet first and have some fun.

ADD VARIETY

Supplement the fabrics in the materials list for the quilt you plan to make with fabrics from your stash. Use a variety of prints to add interest to your quilt.

ASSORTED FABRICS

When the materials list calls for, say 1¼ yards (1.1m) total of assorted fabrics, that means you can choose several solids and/or prints in the same color range to make up the combined yardage total of 1¼ yards (1.1m). You can, of course, use as many different fabrics (or as few!) as you wish to make up the total required, depending on the look you want to achieve.

MISFIT BLOCKS

Don't be afraid to remove a block that isn't working from your quilt. Sometimes a block just doesn't work, and it can take an act of bravery to remove it from the quilt. Be brave! Take that block out, and use it somewhere else. You could use it as the label on the back of the quilt, turn it into a cushion, frame it for the wall or even make a pajama bag!

Some fabrics like corduroy and velvet have a nap, which is the raised pile that runs in one direction. When you are cutting fabric with a nap, there are a couple of things you need to know before you start work on your project to ensure a great outcome:

All of your pattern pieces should face the same direction; otherwise their texture and sometimes even their color will appear to be different. That said, if I want my soft toy to look at bit raggedy and different, I deliberately cut the pieces so the nap runs in a different direction on adjacent pieces. Don't be afraid to throw the rules out the door!

Be careful when ironing fabrics with nap, as you can flatten the pile and leave shiny spots. Use the tip of the iron to press the seam on the wrong side of the fabric rather than using the full base of the iron.

I like to use wool felt in my soft toys. It is easy to cut, doesn't fray and stuffs beautifully. It's strong and durable, yet soft and huggable. Unfortunately, felt doesn't like being machine-washed or dried—it will shrink significantly! If you find your felt toy is in need of cleaning, hand-washing is the best method to use. Simply soak your toy in cold water with a small amount of low-suds washing detergent. Be very gentle; don't scrub, rub or twist. Rinse thoroughly, then place the toy between two towels and squeeze to remove the excess water. Air dry.

Batting

The type of batting that you use for your quilt is a personal choice. It is available in polyester, cotton, wool, bamboo, silk and various blends. Batting is sold in standard precut sizes or by the yard or meter.

When choosing batting for a project, consider how the quilt will be used, whether it will be quilted by hand or machine, how densely it will be quilted and how often the quilt will need to be laundered.

STRETCHY FABRICS

Fabric that has some stretch to it is easier to stuff and more forgiving when you turn your soft toy right side out. But stretch fabrics can be unpredictable so the final size and shape of your soft toy may differ from mine. This variability only makes your soft toy more uniquely yours.

I like to use good quality, preshrunk poly-cotton batting. I need it to be machine washable as I like to throw my quilts in the washing machine on a regular basis to keep them clean and allergen free.

Fusible Webbing and Appliqué Mat

Fusible webbing is a double-sided adhesive paper used for fabric appliqué. When the webbing is placed between two fabrics, the heat of the iron causes the web to melt and fuse the fabrics together. Always read the manufacturer's instructions that come with the fusible web you buy. How hot your iron should be and the fusing times vary between products.

I highly recommend the use of an appliqué mat or Teflon sheet when using fusible web. An appliqué mat will allow you to preassemble the pieces in the correct order and position before fusing them as a single unit to the background block. Once the appliqué has cooled, peel the finished piece off the appliqué mat, position it on the background block, then fuse it in place.

FUSIBLE-WEB APPLIQUÉ

Fusible-web appliqué is a very easy method that allows you to easily add appliqué to quilts and to attach features and embellishments to your soft toys. Follow these steps when using fusible web with your appliqué:

1. Always check your pieces before starting, since they may need to be flipped or reversed before tracing. Sometimes it is necessary to reverse a piece so the design will face in the correct direction. All of the appliqué templates on the CD have been reversed already for ease of use with the fusible webbing.

2. Trace around each piece onto the paper side of the fusible webbing, leaving approximately ½" (1.3cm) between pieces. Cut the pieces out roughly, leaving ¼" (6mm) of paper around the pieces. Do not cut the pieces out on the traced lines.

3. Press the fusible webbing, glue side down, to the wrong side of the fabric you have chosen for your appliqué. When cool, cut the piece out on the traced line.

4. Peel off the backing paper and place the appliqué piece, glue-side down, in position on your project. Use the templates as a guide to position the pieces. The numbers on the templates indicate the order in which the appliqué pieces should be layered. Fuse each piece into place following the manufacturer's instructions.

5. You can leave the edge of the appliqué raw, but I prefer stitching around the appliqué pieces to secure the fabric to the quilt and to give the appliqué a decorative finish.

You can sew around the edges of your appliqué pieces using any decorative edgestitch you want. When I'm stitching around my appliqué, I'm always reminded of the coloring books I had as a child (and now as an adult!) and how the outline defined the shapes. This is how I want my appliqué to look: crisp and outlined, but defined by thread instead of the ink in coloring books.

For machine appliqué, the most common stitches used are straight stitch, zigzag stitch, satin stitch and blanket stitch.

However, my favorite edgestitch is the hand-sewn blanket stitch. I love the texture it gives a project, and the types of thread you can use are endless. Experiment with thread that contrasts with the fabric when stitching around your appliqué; it can add wonderful visual interest to a project. (See the Embroidery Stitch Dictionary later in this chapter for more information on the blanket stitch.)

CAUTION!

Fusible webbing can get very hot and burn your fingers. Always wait for it to cool before cutting it out. If you peel the paper off the piece before it is cool, you may leave some of the adhesive on the backing paper.

FELT & NON-COTTON FABRICS

Use a lower temperature on your iron when fusing on felt and other fabrics that aren't 100% cotton. Read the manufacturer's recommendations first, and test the heat setting on a small fabric swatch before ironing your actual project.

STiTCHiNG TECHNiQUES

Seam Allowance and Sewing Machine Stitches

The seam allowance is the distance between the seam and the cut edge of the fabric. All the quilts in this book are sewn using a ¼" (6mm) seam allowance. Sewing an accurate seam makes all the difference in ensuring your points and seams match up and in giving your quilt a flat, perfect finish.

A ¼" (6mm) seam foot is available for most brands of sewing machine and is highly recommended. For the best results, sew a scant ¼" (6mm) seam as this will allow for the thickness of the thread and the fabric in the pressed seam. Test your seaming by sewing a seam with your ¼" (6mm) foot and then measuring it with a ruler.

A ¼" (6mm) seam allowance is also standard for most soft toy projects. If you are using a fabric that has a loose weave or frays easily, try sewing a wider seam allowance of ⅜" (1cm). A wider seam allowance will make the finished soft toy smaller than stated in the pattern.

I always use a short, straight stitch, a setting of 1.5–1.8, when I'm sewing soft toys on my sewing machine. Using a short stitch length will make your soft toy stronger and more durable. It will also help prevent the seams from ripping or bursting when the soft toy is stuffed.

Use the backstitch on your sewing machine to secure the beginning and the end of a seam. Backstitching your seams, especially at the stuffing openings, will strengthen them and prevent them from coming undone.

Always press your fabric and seams using an up-and-down motion instead of ironing them. Be careful when using the steam setting on your iron as steam can stretch the fabric, particularly edges that are cut on the bias of the fabric.

A basting stitch is essentially the same as a straight stitch except you use a longer stitch length. Use a basting stitch to temporarily hold two fabric pieces or shapes together before stitching the final seam. Once the final seam has been stitched, remove all basting stitches.

Notching the Seams on Soft Toys

When you sew a curve or turn a corner, you will need to notch the seam allowance so the fabric doesn't bunch up when you turn your soft toy right side out. To notch the seam, simply cut little Vs in the seam allowance along the curved edge, cutting from the raw edge of the fabric almost to the seam (Figure 1).

You can achieve the same result by clipping the seam allowance. This simply means that you cut little slits in the fabric instead of Vs. You will need to make several notches or slits in the seam allowance to assure a smooth seam when the soft toy is turned right-side out.

REMOVE PiNS

To avoid damaging your sewing machine or breaking a needle, always remove pins as you sew.

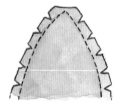

Figure 1

FINISHING YOUR QUILT

Making a Quilt Sandwich

Most quilts are made of three layers: the quilt top, the batting and the backing. How well the three layers are sandwiched together determines whether the finished quilt is wrinkled or puckered.

1. Press the quilt top and backing fabric, and lay out the batting on a flat surface, if necessary, to remove any creases. Trim any stray threads and check to see that your seam allowances are flat.

2. Cut the batting and backing fabric approximately 3" (5.2cm) larger than the quilt top on each side. Lay the backing fabric right-side down on a smooth, flat surface (e.g. the floor). Use masking tape to secure the backing to the surface, keeping it flat and wrinkle free (Figure 1).

3. Place the batting on top of the backing, centering it and smoothing out any wrinkles as you go. Center the pressed quilt on top of the batting and backing, right-side up, and again smooth out any wrinkles (Figure 2).

4. Pin all 3 layers together using safety pins. Start from the center and work your way out toward the edges. You should pin at intervals roughly the width of your hand. The more pins you use, the better the final result will be (Figure 3).

5. Once you have finished pinning the quilt sandwich, gently remove the masking tape, and you are ready to quilt.

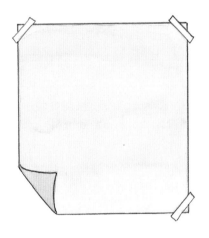

Figure 1

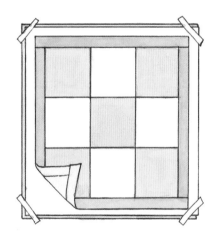

Figure 2

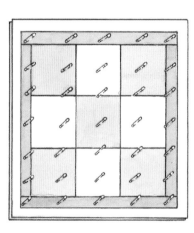

Figure 3

PROFESSIONAL QUILTING

If you have decided to use a professional quilting service, check with them before cutting your batting and backing fabric to size. Each individual service has different requirements about the amount of overhang they need for the batting and backing fabric.

SPRAY ADHESIVES

An alternative to pinning your quilt sandwich together is to use special spray adhesives, available from your local quilt shop. Follow the manufacturer's instructions, and always apply them in an open, airy space.

COMBINE TECHNIQUES

There is no reason why you can't combine machine quilting with hand quilting. Try machine stitching in the seam lines around the edge of your blocks (stitch in the ditch) and around the outside edge of the appliqué pieces, then fill in the background with hand quilting.

MARKING A DESIGN

If you need to mark a quilting design on your quilt top, do this before you make your quilt sandwich. It will be easier than drawing onto the soft quilt sandwich. There are many types of pencils and markers available, but always test them on a scrap of fabric first. If you use an erasable marker, be careful when pressing; the heat of the iron might set the ink and make it impossible to remove.

Quilting

Quilting adds wonderful texture and visual interest to a quilt. Not only does it turn your flimsy quilt top into a warm, squishy, usable quilt, it also secures all three layers to each other and prevents the batting from bunching up.

Quilting can be done by hand, on a domestic sewing machine or by a professional quilting service. How much or how little quilting you do is a personal choice. I prefer my quilts lightly quilted to keep them as soft and cuddly as possible.

Binding Your Quilt

Binding is the final step in completing your project. It creates a neat and secure edge and keeps the quilt sandwich together. The binding on a quilt is like a frame on a painting; it should complement your quilt. Binding doesn't need to be boring—have fun selecting your binding fabric! Experiment with different prints and color schemes to add visual interest.

Try varying the width of your binding. You can make a skinny binding or a wide binding; just remember to adjust the width of your seam allowance to suit the width of the binding.

Scrappy bindings are always fun. Sew a variety of shorter strips together to make one long strip the length of the binding required.

There are several methods for binding the edges of a quilt. The method shown here is my favorite. Instructions for each project in this book include the length and width of the binding strip needed.

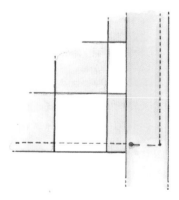

Figure 1

1. Before binding, baste around the outside edges of the quilt, sewing through all layers close to the edge of the quilt top. Trim the batting and backing even with the edges of the quilt top.

2. Sew the binding strips together using diagonal seams until you have 1 long strip. Trim the seam allowances to ¼" (6mm) and press them open. Fold the binding strip in half lengthwise, wrong sides together, and press.

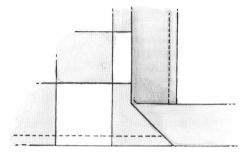

Figure 2

3. Start binding halfway down 1 side of the quilt, aligning the raw edges of the binding and quilt, then pin the binding along the edge. Stitch through all layers using a ¼" (6mm) seam allowance, starting 6" (15.2cm) from the beginning of the binding strip. Stop stitching ¼" (6mm) from the corner and backstitch. Remove the quilt from the sewing machine (Figure 1).

4. Fold the binding strip at a 90° angle (Figure 2). Fold the binding back on itself, aligning the raw edges with the next side of the quilt. The fold will be even with the raw edge of the previously sewn side (Figure 3).

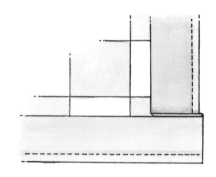

Figure 3

5. Continue sewing the binding to the quilt until you approach the next corner. Sew all sides and corners as previously described, stopping approximately 6" (15.2cm) before the starting point. Remove the quilt from the sewing machine (Figure 4).

6. Bring the tails of the binding together and fold the binding ends back on themselves so the folds just meet. Press the fold to mark the crease. Open the binding strips flat and pin the 2 pieces right sides facing along the creases. Sew along the crease (Figure 5). Trim the seam allowance to ¼" (6mm), press the seam open and refold the binding in half. Pin and then sew the last of the binding to the quilt.

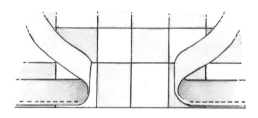

Figure 4

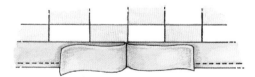

Figure 5

7. Wrap the binding over to the back of the quilt and slipstitch it in place by hand using matching thread. Your stitches should be worked only into the backing fabric and batting, not all the way through to the front of the quilt. The binding can be held in place using pins or binding clips while you sew. Fold the mitered corners into place and secure with neat, tiny stitches (Figure 6).

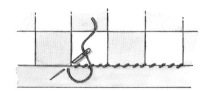

Figure 6

FiNiSHiNG YOUR SOFT TOY

Stuffing Your Soft Toy

This is a very important step in making your soft toy, and it's the one that most of us try to rush. Take your time stuffing your soft toy, use small pieces of stuffing and never cram the stuffing in. Using small pieces of stuffing helps to prevent lumps from forming and keeps your soft toy looking and feeling great for longer.

Your fingers and a ¼" (6mm) wooden dowel or chopstick are the perfect tools for stuffing soft toys. Use the dowel or chopstick to reach the hard-to-get-at, narrow places that your fingers can't reach. Remember to be gentle—you don't want to pop any seams with excessive force. Stuff your soft toy as firmly as your fabric will allow while still maintaining the soft toy's shape.

Ladder Stitch

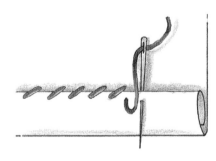

Whip Stitch

Finishing Stitches

Ladder stitch is used to close a stuffing opening in such a way that the stitches are hidden or invisible.

1. Fold in the seam allowances along the opening, matching the folded edges. Press the folds using the tip of your iron.

2. Using a strong polyester sewing thread, thread a hand-sewing needle and knot the ends. Push the needle through the folded edge of 1 seam allowance. The knot will be concealed within the seam as you sew.

3. Stitch into the fold directly opposite your first stitch. The stitch will be concealed in the seam crease.

4. Make another small stitch through the opposite folded edge. Continue stitching in this manner until you reach the end of the opening.

5. When you reach the end of the opening, pull the thread to tighten the stitches. Don't pull too hard or you might snap the thread and have to start again! The stitches will be concealed in the seam and will be almost invisible. Tie off the thread to finish, and bury the knot in the seam.

Whip or overcast stitch is an easy alternative to the ladder stitch, and you may prefer to use this stitch to close stuffing openings. Whip stitch isn't an invisible stitch, so you should always use matching thread and keep your stitches small and neat. I use both stitches when I'm making soft toys, and my choice of stitch usually depends on how lazy I'm feeling!

EMBROIDERY STITCH DICTIONARY

I use a variety of stitches to embellish the projects in this book. All of the stitches are relatively easy to master. This section illustrates how to make the basic stitches recommended in the project instructions.

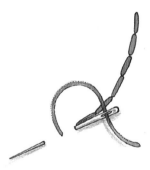

Backstitch

Backstitch is ideal for outlining shapes and stitching straight or curved lines.

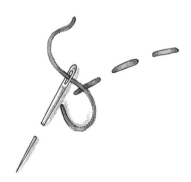

Running Stitch

Running stitch is also ideal for outlining shapes and stitching lines. The stitches are evenly spaced and can run in any direction.

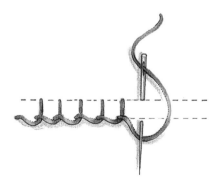

Blanket Stitch

Blanket stitch is a decorative stitch that is usually used to accentuate an edge. It is also used to prevent fraying around the edge of appliqué shapes.

Chainstitch

Chainstitch can be used to stitch lines and curves. It creates a thicker stitching line than backstitch.

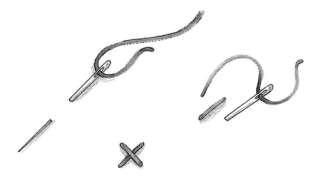

Cross Stitch

A simple cross stitch is used to stitch freckles and belly buttons on the designs.

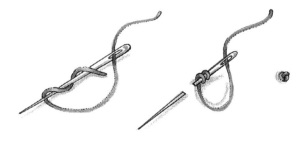

French Knot

French knots are perfect little stitches to use for eyes, freckles and other small details.

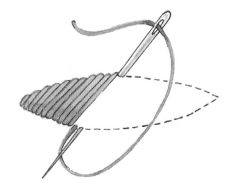

Satin Stitch

Satin stitch is used to fill in areas of a design with long stitches worked side by side. This stitch is perfect to use when replacing button eyes with embroidery.

HOW TO USE THE PATTERN TEMPLATES

All of the templates needed to make the quilts and soft toys are included on the CD-ROM. Print out the PDF of templates for the project you are making on standard letter-size paper. All of the templates are provided at their full size. Make sure that your printer is set to print at 100% with no scaling or cropping.

The appliqué templates provided with this book are reversed for your convenience. The more complex templates are numbered to show the placement order of the pieces. The piece labelled '1' is placed first, followed by piece '2,' '3,' '4,' '5' and so on.

These pieces are also outlined in different colors to make the tracing lines easier to see and trace. Dashed lines indicate where one piece overlaps another, you should continue to trace along these lines. If you choose not to print in color, refer to the color PDF for help distinguishing the pieces.

Always use the template as a guide when positioning the pieces. I recommend using an appliqué mat or Teflon sheet when you are fusing all but the simplest of pieces. A Teflon sheet allows you to preassemble the pieces before fusing the finished piece to the background block.

Remember the appliqué templates are reversed, so when you are using the Teflon sheet to preassemble the appliqué, the pieces will appear to be back-to-front. If you find this confusing, use your computer to reverse the image and print out a second copy.

Some templates are divided into two sections and will need to be joined to create the complete template piece. To do this, match the shapes along the dotted lines, and then use tape to stick them together.

Each project will indicate the number of template pages you need to complete the project so you can make sure you have all the necessary pages printed before you get started.

In addition to the template PDFs, several of the quilt projects include additional layout diagrams to help you see how the various quilt blocks and appliqués come together. These diagrams are not to scale and are for reference only. Do not use them in place of the provided templates.

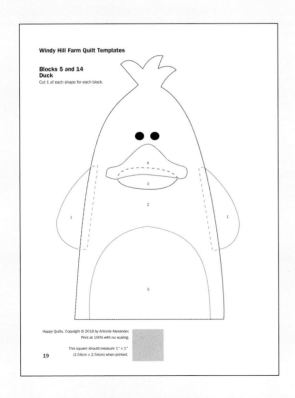

Template page

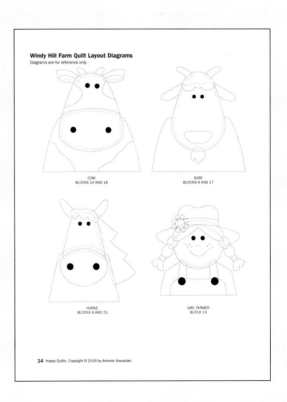

Layout diagram

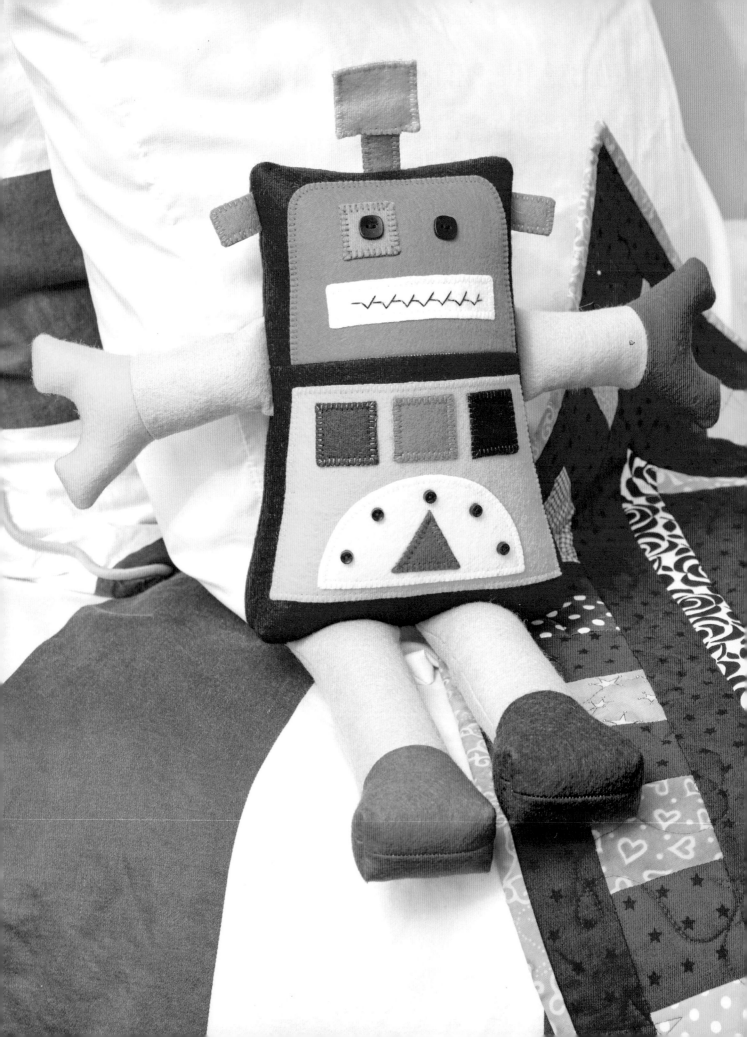

CHAPTER TWO
THE PROJECTS

From a rocketship to the stars and speedy race cars to friendly mer-people and frolicsome kitty cats, the quilts and soft toys in the folliwing pages are ready to take you on an imagintive adventure. Fusibule appliqué and a few simple sewing techniques are all you need to to create these fun, vibrant projects. It's hard not to be happy when you see the joy these quilts and soft toys bring to children of all ages.

HOUND DOGS
QUILT

These happy hound dogs are waiting to be your best friends and bark up a storm. Make a pack of happy Hound Dog Soft Toys, but be sure they don't dig up your garden to bury their tastiest bones!

Finished Size: 56½"× 72½" (143.5cm × 184.2cm)

Materials

Background

½ yard (0.5m) of yellow-on-yellow print fabric

½ yard (0.5m) of yellow & white checked fabric

½ yard (0.5m) of blue-on-blue striped fabric

½ yard (0.5m) of blue & white dot fabric

½ yard (0.5m) of orange-on-orange print fabric

½ yard (0.5m) of denim blue fabric

Border Blocks

½ yard (0.5m) total of assorted blue print and solid fabric

⅜ yard (34cm) total of assorted yellow print and solid fabrics

½ yard (0.5m) total of assorted orange print and solid fabrics

⅜ yard (34cm) total of assorted light cream-on-cream fabrics

Appliqué

1⅜ yards (1.3m) total of assorted brown solid and print fabrics

⅝ yard (0.6m) total of assorted cream solid and print fabrics

Binding and Backing

½ yard (0.5m) of orange-on-orange dot fabric for the binding

4⅜ yards (4m) of fabric for the backing

Assorted Supplies

Light lead pencil

Fabric marking pen

Black embroidery floss for the facial features

Matching thread to suit your favorite method of appliqué

62½" × 78½" (158.8cm × 199.4cm) piece of batting

Approximately 5 yards (4.6m) of lightweight fusible web (I used Heat n Bond Lite, which measures 17" [43cm] wide)

12 pairs of assorted small to medium buttons for the eyes

6 *Hound Dogs Quilt* template pages

Cutting

Background Fabrics

From each of the background fabrics, cut (1) 16½" (41.9cm) × width-of-fabric (WOF) strip. Subcut (2) 16½" (41.9cm) squares for the background of the appliqué blocks (12 squares total).

Border Fabrics: Assorted Blues

Cut (18) 5¼" (13.3cm) squares.

Border Fabrics: Assorted Yellows

Cut (10) 5¼" (13.3cm) squares.

Cut (5) 4½" (11.4cm) squares.

Border Fabrics: Assorted Oranges

Cut (16) 5¼" (13.3cm) squares.

Cut (3) 4½" (11.4cm) squares.

Border Fabrics: Assorted Creams

Cut (9) 5¼" (13.3cm) squares.

Binding Fabric

Cut (7) 2½" (6.4cm) × WOF strips.

Backing Fabric

Cut (2) 78½" (199.4cm) lengths. Remove the selvages.

USE YOUR LEFTOVERS

Use the leftover background fabric for the border blocks and Hound Dog Soft Toy.

Make the Appliqué Blocks

1. Trace the required appliqué pieces from the template pages onto the paper side of the fusible webbing using a sharp pencil; leave approximately ½" (1.3cm) between each piece.

    You will need to trace 12 dog heads (each head is 2 pieces). Trace 4 eye patches, 6 bones, 12 noses, 12 bodies and 12 of each ear. Trace 3 large stars, 2 medium stars and 9 small stars.

2. Cut the pieces out roughly, leaving ¼" (6mm) of paper around each piece. Fuse the pieces to the fabrics you have chosen for the appliqué, following the manufacturer's instructions. Cut the pieces out carefully on the lines when cool.

3. Remove the backing paper from the appliqué pieces and use Figure 1 and the template as a guide to place the dogs on the 16½" (41.9cm) background blocks. The bottom raw edge of the dog's body aligns with the bottom raw edge of the background block.

    When you are happy with the position of the appliqué pieces, fuse them to the background block following the manufacturer's instructions.

4. Stitch around the appliqué pieces using your favorite method. (I used the raw-edge appliqué method when stitching this quilt. To do this, sew around the edge of each piece 2 or 3 times using complementary thread and a straight stitch. Stitch approximately ⅛" (3mm) in from the raw edge of the fabric.)

    Use the template as a guide to draw the mouth on each dog with a fine-point fabric pen. Backstitch each mouth using 2 strands of black embroidery floss.

Figure 1

Make the Quilt Center

1. Lay out the finished dog blocks into 4 rows, each with 3 blocks. When you are happy with the placement of the blocks, sew each horizontal row of 3 blocks together with a ¼" (6mm) seam allowance. Press the seams in each row in opposite directions.

2. Once each row is sewn, pin and then sew the 4 rows together, carefully matching the seams, to make the center of the quilt (Figure 2). Press well and then set aside.

Make the Border Blocks

1. Start with 2 contrasting 5¼" (13.3cm) squares. Cut each square twice on the diagonal to make 4 quarter-square triangles (Figure 3). This will make 2 blocks.

2. Lay out the quarter-square triangles to form the block. Use a ¼" (6mm) seam to sew the triangles together in pairs; then sew the pairs together to make a block (Figure 4). Repeat to make 52 blocks. Refer to the photo at the end of this project as guide to color choices and placement. You will have 4 leftover quarter triangles. Discard them or save them for another project.

3. Center and fuse a small star to each of the eight 4½" (11.4cm) squares. Stitch around the appliqué pieces as before.

STABLE BLOCKS

A spritz of spray starch before pressing will add stability to the blocks.

Figure 2

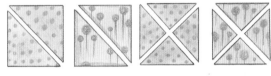

Figure 3

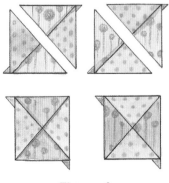

Figure 4

ADJUSTING BORDERS

The length of the borders can be adjusted as needed by stitching random seams along the border wider or narrower.

Make the Borders

1. To make the side borders, sew 14 quarter-square triangle blocks and 2 star blocks together end to end. Insert the 2 star blocks randomly in the strip. Make 2 borders, each measuring 64½" (163.8cm) long. Sew a border to each side of the quilt. Press the seams outward.

2. To make the top and bottom borders, sew 12 quarter-square triangle blocks and 2 star blocks together end to end. Insert the 2 star blocks randomly in the strip. Make 2 borders, each measuring 56½" (143.5cm) long. Sew a border to the top and bottom of the quilt. Press the seams outward.

Finish the Appliqué

1. Randomly place and fuse the 3 large stars, 2 medium stars and 1 small star to the quilt top. Stitch around the appliqué pieces as before.

Prepare the Backing

1. Sew the two 78½" (199.4cm) lengths of backing fabric together along the long edges, then trim to make a piece measuring approximately 62½" × 78½" (158.8cm × 199.4cm).

Finish the Quilt

1. Layer the backing, batting and quilt top (see Making a Quilt Sandwich on page 15). Baste the layers together using your favorite method. Start quilting from the center and work your way out to the edges.

2. Sew the 7 binding strips together using diagonal seams. Trim the seams to ¼" (6mm) and press them open. Fold the binding strip in half lengthwise, wrong sides facing, and press well.

    Sew the binding to the front of the quilt using a ¼" (6mm) seam, and then sew the ends together where they meet. Wrap the binding to the back of the quilt and handstitch in place.

3. Sew buttons to the dogs' faces for eyes where indicated on the template. Sew the buttons in place through all thicknesses of the quilt using strong thread. Knot securely. Label and date your quilt to finish.

HOUND DOG
SOFT TOY

Finished Size: 20" (50.8cm) tall

Materials

1 fat eighth (45.7 × 27.9cm) of brown wool felt for the head

4" × 7" (10.2cm × 17.2cm) rectangle of orange & white dot fabric for the ears

9" (22.9cm) square of blue-on-blue striped fabric for the ears and body

8" (20.3cm) square of brown-on-brown checked fabric for the ears

8" (20.3cm) square of brown & cream plaid fabric for the muzzle and tail

4" × 3" (10.2cm × 7.6cm) rectangle of black wool felt for the nose

8" (20.3cm) square of brown & white dot fabric for the arms

8" (20.3cm) square of brown-on-brown floral print fabric for the arms

10" (25.4cm) square each of 2 brown plaid fabrics for the legs

5" × 8" (12.7cm × 20.3cm) rectangle of orange small-print fabric for the body

5" × 8" (12.7cm × 20.3cm) rectangle of orange-on-orange striped fabric for the body

5" × 8" (12.7cm × 20.3cm) rectangle of blue & white dot fabric for the body

3½" × 12" (8.9cm × 30.5cm) rectangle of yellow & white checked fabric for the collar

2" × 4" (5.1cm × 10.2cm) rectangle of white wool felt for the dog tag

Assorted Supplies

Light lead pencil

Fabric marking pen

Matching thread suit your favorite method of appliqué

Black embroidery floss for the facial features

3½" × 12" (8.9cm × 30.5cm) rectangle of lightweight fusible interfacing for the collar

7" (17.8cm) square of lightweight fusible web

Temporary fabric basting glue (I used Roxanne's Temporary Basting Glue)

1 large cream button for the eyes

2 small black buttons for the eyes

1 small green button for the collar

Polyester fiberfill

Tracing paper (optional)

4 *Hound Dog Soft Toy* template pages

Cutting

Trace and cut out the template pieces. You will need to trace the head, ear, body, arm, leg, tail and dog tag pieces. Pin the template pieces to the fabrics you have chosen and cut the following:

Orange Fabric

Cut 2 body pieces.

Blue Fabric

Cut 2 body pieces (both cut in reverse).

Cut 1 ear piece.

Brown Fabric

Cut 2 ear pieces.

Orange & White Dot Fabric

Cut 1 ear piece.

Brown & White Dot Fabric

Cut 2 arm pieces (cut 1 in reverse).

Brown-on-Brown Print Fabric

Cut 2 arm pieces (cut 1 in reverse).

Brown Plaid Fabrics

Cut 2 leg pieces from each of the 2 brown plaid fabrics (cut 1 in reverse in each fabric).

Brown Plaid Fabrics

Cut 2 tail pieces (cut 1 in reverse).

Brown Felt

Cut 2 head pieces (cut 1 in reverse).

Yellow & White Checked Fabric

Cut (2) 1½" × 11" (3.8cm × 27.9cm) rectangles for the collar.

Interfacing

Cut (1) 1" × 10½" (2.5cm × 26.7cm) rectangle for the collar.

White Felt

Cut 2 dog tag pieces.

Figure 1

Make the Hound Dog

Note: A short 1.5 stitch length and a ¼" (6mm) seam are used throughout.

1. Trace the muzzle and nose pieces from the template pages onto the paper side of the fusible webbing using a sharp pencil; leave approximately ½" (1.3cm) between each piece. Cut the pieces out roughly, leaving ¼" (6mm) of paper around each piece.

2. Fuse the muzzle to the brown & cream plaid fabric and the nose to the black felt following the manufacturer's instructions. Cut the pieces out carefully on the lines when cool. Remove the backing paper from the appliqué pieces and use the template as a guide to fuse them to the front head piece.

3. Stitch around the appliqué pieces using your favorite method. (I used blanket-stitch and 2 strands of coordinating embroidery floss.) Draw the mouth on the muzzle and chainstitch using 2 strands of black embroidery floss. Sew the buttons to the face for eyes using strong thread, then knot securely (Figure 1). Note: The black button is placed on top of the white button to create an eye patch.

4. Sew the ear pieces together in pairs, a brown ear to a colored ear, with right sides facing. Leave the bottom edge open as marked on the template.

   Notch the seam allowances on the curves and turn the ears right-side out through the opening. Press gently. Fold the bottom edges of the ears inward approximately ¼" (6mm) on each side. Pin and then baste in place (Figure 2).

5. Use the template as a guide to position the ears, colored sides down and facing inwards, on the appliquéd head piece. Pin and then baste them to the face (Figure 3).

6. Sew a blue and an orange body piece together with right sides facing. Press the seam open (Figure 4). This is the front body piece.

7. Pin and then sew the front head piece to the front body piece with right sides facing (Figure 5). Press the seam downward. Set this aside.

8. Sew the tail pieces together with right sides facing. Leave the bottom edge open where marked on the template. Notch the seam allowances on the curves and turn the tail right-side out through the opening. Add a pinch of stuffing to the tail to make it soft and squishy.

   Use the template as a guide to position the tail on 1 of the remaining body pieces with the raw edges aligned. Pin and then baste the tail to the back body piece (Figure 6).

Figure 2

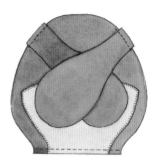

Figure 3

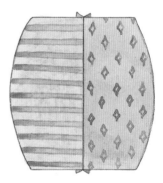

Figure 4

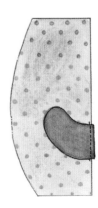

Figure 6

Figure 5

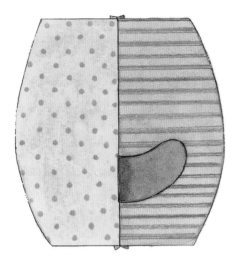

Figure 7

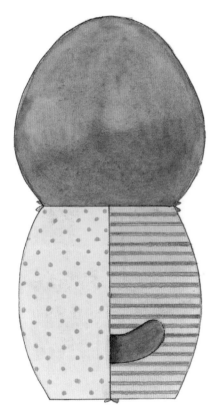

Figure 8

9. Sew the 2 back body pieces together with right sides facing. Leave the seam open as marked on the template. Press the seam open (Figure 7).

   Pin and then sew the back head piece to the back body piece with right sides facing (Figure 8). Press the seam downward.

10. Sew the arms together in pairs with right sides facing. Leave the top and side seams open as marked on the template. Notch the seam allowances on the curves and turn the arms right-side out through the top opening.

11. Sew the legs together in the same manner. Notch the seam allowances on the curves and turn the legs right-side out through the top opening.

12. Place the front of the dog right-side up on your work surface. Use the template as a guide to position the arms and legs right sides down and facing inward on the body. Make sure the stuffing openings are facing downward on the arms and inward on the legs. Pin and then baste them to the dog (Figure 9). The arms and legs are not stuffed until the dog is completed.

Figure 9

13. Place the front of the dog right-side up on your work surface again. Fold the arms, legs and ears in toward the center of the body. Place the back body piece on top of the front body piece with the right side facing down. Pin the pieces together well to secure (Figure 10). Sew around the dog using a short stitch length, being careful to catch only the basted ends of the arms, legs and ears in the seams.

14. Carefully notch the seam allowance on the curves, then gently turn the dog right-side out through the back opening. Stuff the body, arms and legs until firm. Hand-stitch the openings closed.

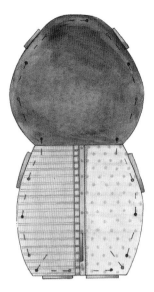

Figure 10

Make the Collar and Tag

1. Center the strip of interfacing on the wrong side of 1 yellow & white checked collar piece. Iron it in place following the manufacturer's instructions.

2. Place the 2 yellow & white checked collar pieces together with right sides facing. The interfacing will be facing outward. Sew down both long edges and 1 short end using a scant ¼" (6mm) seam.

   Trim the corners and turn the collar right-side out and press gently. Neaten the collar by tucking the raw ends inwards approximately ¼" (6mm) and press in place (Figure 11). Topstitch close to the edge around all 4 sides of the collar. Press well.

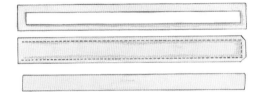

Figure 11

3. Use a spot of basting glue to "pin" the white felt dog tags together. Blanket-stitch around the edges of the dog tags, sewing through the 2 layers of felt. When you have finished, knot the thread and bury it in the felt.

4. Find the center of the collar and pin the dog tag in place. Sew a green button to the dog tag, stitching through the dog tag and the collar to secure (Figure 12).

   Place the collar around the Hound Dog's neck and hand-stitch the ends together using small stitches.

Figure 12

THE DEEP BLUE SEA
QUILT

Let the seaweed tickle your toes as you have a magical underwater adventure in the deep blue sea. Swim with jewel-bright fish and your new friends as you discover the wonderful world of make-believe.

Finished Size: 55½" × 55½" (141cm × 141cm)

Materials

Background and Borders
3½ yards (3.2m) total of assorted blue-on-blue print and blue-on-blue batik fabrics

⅜ yard (34cm) total of green-on-green print fabrics for the seaweed blocks

Appliqué
1¼ yard (1.1m) total of assorted yellow print fabrics, orange print fabrics, red print fabrics, pink print fabrics and green print fabrics

12" (30.5cm) square each of solid white and solid black fabric for the eyes

Binding and Backing
½ yard (0.5m) of yellow & blue dot fabric for the binding

3½ yards (3.2m) of fabric for the backing

Assorted Supplies
Light lead pencil

Fabric marking pen (fine-point)

Black embroidery floss for the facial features

Matching thread to suit your favorite method of appliqué

61½" × 61½" (156.2cm × 156.2cm) piece of batting

Approximately 3 yards (2.7m) of lightweight fusible web (I used Heat n Bond Lite, which measures 17" [43cm] wide)

4 *Deep Blue Sea Quilt* template pages

Cutting

Assorted Blue Fabrics

Cut (33) 7½" (19.1cm) squares for the background of the fish blocks.

Cut (16) 9½" (24.1cm) squares for the seaweed blocks.

Cut (28) 3½" × 7½" (8.9cm × 19.1cm) rectangles for the border.

Cut (4) 3½" (8.9cm) squares for the border.

Assorted Green-on-Green Print Fabrics

Cut (21) 1½" × 12½" (3.8cm × 31.8cm) strips.

Yellow & Blue Dot Fabric

Cut (6) 3" (7.6cm) × WOF strips for the binding.

Backing Fabric

Cut (2) 61½" (156.2cm) lengths. Remove the selvages.

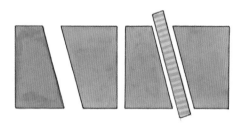

Figure 1

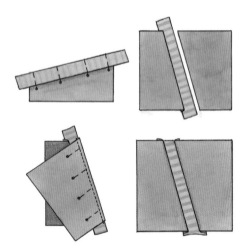

Figure 2

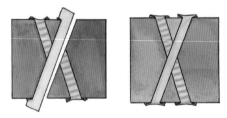

Figure 3

Make the Seaweed Blocks

1. Place a 9½" (24.1cm) blue background square right-side up on your cutting mat. Use your ruler and rotary cutter to make 1 diagonal cut through the center of the fabric. Place a 1½" × 12½" (3.8cm × 31.8cm) green fabric strip right-side up in between the 2 background pieces (Figure 1).

2. Sew the 3 pieces together, with right sides facing, using ¼" (6mm) seams. Press the seams toward the green fabric. Repeat to make 16 single-strip seaweed blocks. Trim 11 blocks evenly on all sides to measure 7½" (19.1cm) square. Set aside (Figure 2).

3. Use the remaining 5 blocks to make the double-strip seaweed blocks. Place an untrimmed single seaweed block right-side up on your cutting mat. Trim the over-hanging strips of green fabric even with the edges of the block. Use your ruler to make a second diagonal cut through the block.

4. Place a 1½" × 12½" (3.8cm × 31.8cm) green strip in between the 2 pieces. Sew them together in the same manner as before. Line up the top edges of the block when you are sewing it together, and don't worry if the seaweed strips don't align perfectly. Press the seams toward the green fabric. Trim the block evenly on all sides to measure 7½" (19.1cm) square (Figure 3). Repeat to make 5 double seaweed blocks in total.

5. Pin and then sew a 7½" (19.1cm) blue background square to a single seaweed block. Leave the seams unpressed. Repeat to make 5 joined blocks (Figure 4).

   Repeat to sew 5 blue background squares to 5 double seaweed blocks (Figure 5). Set aside.

Make the Appliqué Blocks

1. Trace the required appliqué pieces from the template pages onto the paper side of the fusible webbing using a sharp pencil; leave approximately ½" (1.3cm) between each piece.

   You will need to trace 5 of Fish A, 5 of Fish B, 8 of Fish C and 15 of Fish D including their eyes.

   Refer to the photo at the end of this project as a guide to color choices and orientation of the blocks throughout the project.

2. Cut the fish out roughly, leaving ¼" (6mm) of paper around each piece. Fuse the fish to the fabrics you have chosen for the appliqué, following the manufacturer's instructions. Cut the fish out carefully on the lines when cool.

3. Remove the backing paper from the 23 small fish. Center them on the remaining 7½" (19.1cm) blue background blocks (Figure 6). When you are happy with the orientation of the fish, fuse them to the background blocks following the manufacturer's instructions.

4. Stitch around the appliqué pieces using your favorite method. (I used hand-stitched blanket stitch and 2 strands of matching embroidery flloss.) Use the template as a guide to draw the smile on each fish using a fine-point fabric pen. Backstitch each smile using 2 strands of black embroidery floss (Figure 6). Set aside.

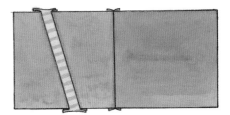

Figure 4

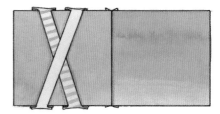

Figure 5

Figure 6

SERIOUS FISH

Leave some fish without smiles for variation.

Figure 7

Figure 8

Figure 9

WiDE BiNDING

When sewing the wide 3" (7.6cm) binding to the quilt, remember to stop ½" (1.3cm) from the corner instead of ¼" (6mm) to match your seam allowance.

Make the Quilt Center

1. Use Figure 7 as a guide to lay out the fish blocks and the seaweed blocks (including the joined seaweed blocks) into 7 rows each with 7 blocks. When you are happy with the orientation of the blocks, sew each horizontal row of blocks together and press the seams in each row in opposite directions.

2. Remove the backing paper from the 10 large fish and use the photo at the end of this project as a guide to fuse them to the remaining blank background blocks. The large fish will overlap the seam between the blank background blocks and the seaweed blocks. Ensure the fish are facing the correct direction. Stitch around the fish using your favorite method. Stitch their smiles as before.

3. Lay out the 7 rows of blocks again. When you are happy with the orientation of the rows, pin and then sew the 7 rows together, carefully matching the seams, to make the center of the quilt. Press well.

Make the Borders

1. To make the side borders, sew 7 assorted blue 3½" × 7½" (8.9cm × 19.1cm) rectangles together end to end. Make 2 borders, each measuring 49½" (125.7cm) long (Figure 8). Sew a border to each side of the quilt. Press the seams outward.

2. To make the top and bottom borders, sew 7 assorted blue rectangles together in the same manner, then sew a 3½" (8.9cm) square to each end. Make 2 borders, each measuring 55½" (141cm) long (Figure 9). Sew a border to the top and bottom of the quilt. Press the seams outward.

Prepare the Backing

1. Sew the two 61½" (156.2cm) lengths of backing fabric together along the long edges, then trim to make a piece measuring approximately 61½" (156.2cm) square.

Finish the Quilt

1. Layer the backing, batting and quilt top (see Making a Quilt Sandwich on page 15). Baste the layers together using your favorite method. Start quilting from the center and work your way out to the edges.

2. Sew the 6 binding strips together using diagonal seams. Trim the seams to ¼" (6mm) and press them open. Fold the binding strip in half lengthwise, wrong sides facing, and press well. Sew the binding to the front of the quilt using a ½" (1.3cm) seam, and then sew the ends together where they meet. Wrap the binding to the back of the quilt and hand-stitch in place. Label and date your quilt to finish.

DEEP BLUE SEA
SOFT TOY

Finished Size: 19" (48.3cm) tall

Materials

For the Mermaid

14" × 17" (35.6cm × 43.2cm) rectangle of skin-colored wool felt for the face, body and arms

12" (30.5cm) square of bright pink wool felt for the hair

9" × 13" (22.9cm × 33cm) rectangle of bright blue wool felt for the tail

7" × 8" (17.8cm × 20.3cm) rectangle of bright green & white large dot fabric for the flipper

8" × 12" (20.3cm × 30.5cm) rectangle of blue & green checked fabric for the bikini top

2 small black buttons for the eyes

Pearl beads for necklace (optional)

Small yellow silk flower with white button center (optional)

For the Merboy

14" × 17" (35.6cm × 43.2cm) rectangle of skin-colored wool felt for the face, ears, body and arms

7" × 11" (17.8cm × 27.9cm) rectangle of blue-green wool felt for the hair

9" × 13" (45.7cm × 27.9cm) rectangle of bright royal blue wool felt for the tail

7" × 8" (17.8cm × 20.3cm) rectangle of blue & green checked fabric for the flipper

2 small black button for the eyes

DK weight yarn in green and blue, plus US size 4 knitting needles for scarf (optional)

Pearl beads for scarf (optional)

Assorted Supplies (for both dolls)

Light lead pencil

Fabric marking pen

Raspberry red and skin-colored embroidery floss for the facial features

Scraps of felt in 4 different colors for the stars

11" (27.9cm) square of lightweight fusible web

9" × 7" (22.9cm × 17.8cm) rectangle of batting

Polyester fiberfill

Tracing paper (optional)

5 *Deep Blue Sea Soft Toy* template pages

Cutting for the Mermaid

Trace and cut out the template pieces. You will need to trace the head, body, arm, tail and flipper pieces. Pin the template pieces to the fabrics you have chosen and cut the following:

Skin-Colored Felt

Cut 1 face piece, 2 body pieces (cut 1 in reverse) and 4 arm pieces (cut 2 in reverse).

Pink Felt

Cut 1 head piece in reverse.

Cut (1) 5" × 5½" (12.7m × 14cm) rectangle for the hair.

Blue Felt

Cut 2 tail pieces (cut 1 in reverse).

Green & White Dot Fabric

Cut 2 flipper pieces (cut 1 in reverse).

Batting

Cut 1 flipper piece.

Blue & Green Checked Fabric

Cut (1) 2¼" × 6½" (5.7cm × 16.5cm) rectangle for the bikini back.

Cut (4) 2¼" × 7½" (5.7cm × 19.1cm) rectangles for the bikini front.

Cutting for the Merboy

To make the merboy, cut 4 ears (2 in reverse) from the skin-colored felt. Cut the hair, tail and flipper from the appropriate colors. See page 47 for more details.

Make the Mermaid

Note: A short 1.5 stitch length and a ¼" (6mm) seam are used throughout.

1. Trace 1 front hair piece and 4 stars from the template pages onto the paper side of the fusible webbing using a sharp pencil; leave approximately ½" (1.3cm) between each piece. Cut the pieces out roughly, leaving ¼" (6mm) of paper around each piece.

2. Fuse the hair piece to the pink felt and the stars to the assorted scraps of felt, following the manufacturer's instructions. Cut the pieces out carefully on the lines when cool. Set the stars aside. Remove the backing paper and use the template as a guide to fuse the hair to the front head piece.

3. Stitch around the edge of the hairline using your favorite appliqué method. (I used a machine straight stitch with coordinating thread.)

   Draw the mouth, nose and belly button on the doll. Chainstitch the mouth using 2 strands of raspberry red embroidery floss. Backstitch the nose and satin-stitch the belly button using 2 strands of skin-colored embroidery floss. Sew the buttons to the face for eyes with strong thread. Knot securely. (Figure 1).

4. Pin and then sew the front head piece to the front body piece with right sides facing. Press the seams open. Set this aside.

Figure 1

5. Take the pink felt rectangle you are using for the hair and stitch 6 rectangles measuring approximately ½" × 4½" (1.3cm × 11.4cm) directly onto the pink felt, leaving ¼" (6mm) between each rectangle (Figure 2). Cut the rectangles out, cutting close to the stitching lines (Figure 3).

6. Fold each strip of pink felt in half to form a loop. Place 3 loops side by side, the raw ends of each loop overlapping the other slightly. Use the template as a guide to position the hair on the right side of the back head piece. The loops will face inward. Leave approximately ¼" (6mm) overhang on the hair. Pin and then baste the hair in place. Repeat for the opposite side of the head (Figure 4).

7. Pin and then sew the back head piece to the back body piece with right sides facing. Press the seams open. Set this aside.

8. Press under a ¼" (6mm) hem on each long edge of the 2¼" × 6½" (5.7cm × 16.5cm) blue & green checked rectangle. Use the template as a guide to pin it, right side facing up, on the back body piece. The short ends of the bikini will overlap the sides of the body. Topstitch close to the edge on both long edges of the bikini using matching thread. Trim the edges of the bikini to match the back body piece (Figure 5).

9. Sew the remaining four 2¼" × 7½" (5.7cm × 19.1cm) blue & green checked rectangles together in pairs with right sides facing. Leave 1 short end open on each pair for turning. Carefully clip the corners and turn each piece right-side out. Press well, then topstitch close to the edges using matching thread to neaten.

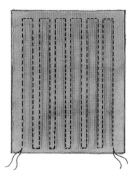

Figure 2

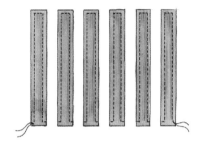

Figure 3

Figure 4

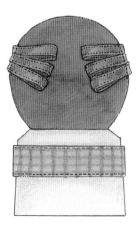

Figure 5

Figure 6   Figure 7

Figure 8   Figure 9

Figure 10

10. Place the front of the doll right-side up on your work surface. Use the template as a guide to position the bikini pieces facing inward on the body. Pin and then baste the 2 bikini pieces to the front body piece with raw edges matching. Angle the bikini slightly upward (Figure 6).

11. Sew the arms together in pairs with right sides facing. Leave the top and side seams open where marked on the template. Carefully notch the seam allowances on the curves and turn the arms right side-out through the top opening.

12. Place the front of the doll right-side up on your work surface. Use the template as a guide to position the arms right sides down and facing inward on the body. Make sure the stuffing openings are facing downward on the arms. Pin and then baste them to the doll (Figure 7). The arms are not stuffed until the doll is completed. Set aside.

13. Place the 2 green & white dot flipper pieces right sides facing then place the flipper piece cut from the batting on top. Pin and then sew them together, leaving the top edge open. Carefully notch the seam allowances and turn the flipper right-side out. Press well. Use a sharp pencil to draw the topstitching lines on the flipper. Topstitch on the marked lines using matching thread (Figure 8).

14. Center and baste the flipper to 1 tail piece with right sides facing. Leave approximately a ¼" (6mm) seam allowance on each side of the flipper (Figure 9).

15. Pin and then sew the tail/flipper piece to front of the doll with right sides facing. Press the seam open. Repeat to sew the remaining tail piece to the back of the doll (Figure 10).

Remove the backing paper from the 4 stars and use the photo as a guide to fuse them to the front of the tail. Stitch around the stars as before.

BULKY SEAMS

Trim any bulky (felt) seams close to the seam line, approximately ⅛" (3mm).

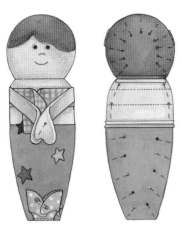

Figure 11

Figure 12

STRENGTHEN SEAMS

Backstitch at the beginning and end of each seam to strengthen the stitching.

USE SAFETY PINS

When pinning the front and back of the doll together, use safety pins to secure the arms, bikini and flipper in place. This will stop them from unfolding and getting caught in the seams.

16. Place the front of the doll right-side up on your work surface. Fold the arms, bikini and flipper in toward the center of the body. Place the of the doll on top of the front of the doll with right sides facing, taking care to tuck the hair in toward the center of the doll. Pin the shapes together well to secure (Figure 11). Sew around the doll using a short stitch length, leaving an opening on the side of the tail as marked on the template. Be very careful to catch only the basted ends of the hair, arms, bikini and flipper in the seams as you sew.

17. Carefully notch the seams on the curves and then turn the doll right-side out through the side opening. Stuff the body and arms until firm. Hand-stitch the openings closed.

18. Knot the bikini ties, then string some pearl beads onto strong thread and secure them around the mermaid's neck. Stitch a silk flower to her hair to finish.

Make the Merboy

1. Follow the steps for the mermaid, omitting steps 8–10 for the bikini top.

2. Instead of making the mermaid's hair in steps 6–7, make ears: Sew the ears together in pairs with right sides facing. Notch the seam allowances on the curves, then turn the ears right-side out. Use the template as a guide to pin and then baste them to the back head piece (Figure 12).

3. If you wish to give your merboy a scarf, cast 12 stitches onto size 4 needles using DK weight yarn. Knit in stockinette stitch, adding stripes every 12 rows, until the scarf measures approximately 16" (40.6cm) in length. Bind off, then sew pearl beads to the scarf using strong thread. Tie the scarf around his neck to finish.

BEDTIME SUPERHEROES
QUILT

Don your mask and cape and help the superheroes protect your blanket fortress from bedtime supervillains. Be very careful not to reveal your secret identity to anyone...sssh!

Finished Size: 58½" × 58½" (148.6cm × 148.6cm)

Materials

Background Blocks

⅜ yard (34cm) each of 5 different background fabrics: gray-on-gray dot fabric (A); gray & white tiny checked fabric (B); gray & white small checked fabric (C); gray & white thin striped fabric (D); and gray & white large dot fabric (F)

¾ yard (0.7m) of gray & white medium chevron fabric (E)

Cornerstones

5" (12.7cm) × WOF of white-on-white fabric

Appliqué and Sashing Strips

½ yard (0.5m) total of assorted print and solid fabrics in each of the following colors: green, red, orange, black and blue

⅜ yard (34cm) total of assorted print and solid fabrics in each of the following colors: yellow, pink and purple

¼ yard (23cm) total of assorted white-on-white fabrics

Scraps of assorted solid gray and gray-on-gray fabrics

8" (20.3cm) square of solid brown fabric

Fifteen 10" (25.4cm) squares of assorted solid skin-toned fabrics including 2 solid green fabrics

Binding and Backing

½ yard (0.5m) of black & white striped fabric for the binding

3⅝ yards (3.3m) of fabric for the backing

Assorted Supplies

Light lead pencil

Fabric marking pen

Brown and black embroidery floss for the facial features

Matching thread to suit your favorite method of appliqué

64½" (163.8cm) square of batting

Approximately 5½ yards (5m) of lightweight fusible web (I use Heat n Bond Lite, which measures 17" (43cm) wide)

14 pairs of assorted small button for the eyes

1 extra black button for an eye

5 assorted medium buttons for the capes

30 *Bedtime Superheroes Quilt* template pages

Cutting

Background Fabrics

From each of the background fabrics A, B, C, D and F cut (1) 12½" (31.8cm) × WOF strip.

From Fabric A, subcut (2) 12½" (31.8cm) squares.

From Fabric B, subcut (3) 12½" (31.8cm) squares.

From Fabric C, subcut (3) 12½" (31.8cm) squares.

From Fabric D, subcut (2) 12½" (31.8cm) squares.

From Fabric F, subcut (2) 12½" (31.8cm) squares.

From Fabric E, cut (2) 12½" (31.8cm) × WOF strips. Subcut (4) 12½" (31.8cm) squares.

Cornerstones

Cut (2) 2½" (6.4cm) × WOF strips. Subcut (25) 2½" (6.4cm) squares.

Sashing Strips

Cut 2½" × 12½" (6.4cm × 31.8cm) rectangles from from the following fabrics: 7 red rectangles, 6 green rectangles, 8 orange rectangles, 7 blue rectangles, 4 yellow rectangles, 4 pink rectangles and 4 purple rectangles.

Binding Fabric

Cut (6) 3" (7.6cm) × WOF strips.

Backing Fabric

Cut (2) 64½" (163.8cm) lengths. Remove the selvages.

Figure 1

Make the Appliqué Blocks

1. Trace the required appliqué pieces from the template pages onto the paper side of the fusible webbing using a sharp pencil; leave approximately ½" (1.3cm) between each piece.

   You will need to trace 16 complete superheroes.

2. Cut the pieces out roughly, leaving ¼" (6mm) of paper around each piece. Fuse the piece to the fabrics you have chosen for the appliqué, following the manufacturer's instructions. Cut the pieces out carefully on the lines when cool.

3. Remove the backing paper from the appliqué pieces and use Figure 1 and the templates as a guide to place the superheroes on the background blocks. The bottom raw edge of the body (and cape, where applicable) aligns with the bottom raw edge of the background block.

   When you are happy with the position of the appliqué pieces, fuse them to the background block following the manufacturer's instructions.

4. Stitch around the appliqué pieces using your favorite method (I used a machine blanket stitch). Use the template as a guide to draw the features on each superhero with a fine-point fabric pen. Backstitch the features using 2 strands of black or brown embroidery floss.

Make the Quilt Center

1. Lay out the finished superhero blocks into 4 rows, each with 4 blocks. Refer to the photo at the end of this project as a guide to color choices and placement throughout the project. When you are happy with the placement of the blocks, sew each horizontal row together, adding the 2½" × 12½" (6.4cm × 31.8cm) assorted sashing strips between the blocks and on the outside edges of each row. Press the seams toward the sashing strips (Figure 2).

2. Sew the remaining 2½" × 12½" (6.4cm × 31.8cm) assorted rectangles and the 2½" (6.4cm) white-on-white squares together at the short ends, alternating them as you sew, to make making 5 sashing strips. Each sashing strip consists of 4 rectangles and 5 squares. Press the seams toward the rectangles (Figure 3).

3. Lay out the 4 rows of blocks on a flat surface again. Place the long sashing strips in between and on the top and bottom of the rows (Figure 4). When you are happy with the placement of the rows, pin and then sew them together, carefully matching the seams, to make the quilt top. Press well.

Figure 2

Figure 3

Figure 4

Prepare the Backing

1. Sew the two 64½" (163.8cm) lengths of backing fabric together along the long edges, then trim to make a piece measuring approximately 64½"(163.8cm) square.

Finish the Quilt

1. Layer the backing, batting and quilt top (see Making a Quilt Sandwich on page 15). Baste the layers together using your favorite method. Start quilting from the center and work your way out to the edges.

2. Sew the 6 binding strips together using straight seams (using straight seams will allow the stripe pattern to run along the binding uninterrupted). Press the seams open. Fold the binding strip in half lengthwise, wrong sides facing, and press well.

3. Sew the binding to the front of the quilt using a ½" (1.3cm) seam, and then sew the ends together where they meet. Wrap the binding to the back of the quilt and hand-stitch in place.

4. Sew buttons to the faces for eyes and to their capes where indicated on the pattern templates. Sew the buttons in place through all thicknesses of the quilt using strong thread. Knot securely. Label and date your quilt to finish.

BEDTIME SUPERHERO SOFT TOY

Finished Size: 22" (55.9cm) tall

Materials

7½" × 12½" (19.1cm × 31.8cm) rectangle of orange wool felt for the hair

10" × 14½" (25.4cm × 36.8cm) rectangle of skin-colored wool felt for the face, ears and hands

1 fat quarter (45.7cm × 55.9cm) of solid blue fabric for the cape

11½" × 16" (29.2cm × 40.6cm) rectangle of red & white star print fabric for the cape lining

1 fat eighth (45.7cm × 27.9cm) of gray & white small checked fabric for the shirt

1 fat quarter (45.7cm × 55.9cm) of denim blue fabric for the pants

7" (17.8cm) square of black wool felt for the mask

3" × 6" (7.6cm × 15.2cm) rectangle of white wool felt for the mask eyes

2" × 12" (5.1cm × 30.5cm) rectangle of solid bright yellow fabric for the belt

3½" × 7½" (8.9cm × 19.1cm) rectangle of a second solid bright yellow fabric for the cape lightning bolt

2" × 4½" (5.1cm × 11.4cm) rectangle of green-on-green fabric for the belt

4" × 6" (10.2cm × 15.2cm) rectangle of white-on-white fabric for the shield

Assorted Supplies

Light lead pencil

Fabric marking pen

Brown embroidery floss for the facial features

Matching thread to suit your favorite method of appliqué

14" (35.6cm) square of lightweight fusible web

4 small black buttons for the eyes

Polyester fiberfill

Large-eyed hand sewing needle

10" (25.4cm) piece of black elastic thread

Tracing paper (optional)

7 *Bedtime Superhero Soft Toy* template pages

SUPER GIRL

To make a girl superhero, use the hair templates from the *Tiny Princess Soft Toy*. You will need 16" (40.6cm) of felt.

Cutting

Trace and cut out the template pieces. You will need to trace the head, ears, front body, back body, arm, hand, leg, pants, cape and mask eye pieces. Pin the template pieces to the fabrics you have chosen and cut the following:

Gray & White Small Checked Fabric

Cut 1 front body piece.

Cut 2 back body pieces (cut 1 in reverse).

Cut 4 arm pieces (cut 2 in reverse).

Skin-Colored Felt

Cut 1 head piece.

Cut 4 ear pieces (cut 2 in reverse).

Cut 4 hand pieces (cut 2 in reverse).

Orange Felt

Cut 1 head piece in reverse.

Denim Fabric

Cut 2 pant pieces.

Cut 4 leg pieces (cut 2 in reverse).

Solid Blue Fabric

Cut (1) 2" × 20½" (5.1cm × 50.8cm) strip for the cape ties.

Cut 1 cape piece on the fold.

Red & White Star Fabric

Cut 1 cape piece on the fold for the lining.

White Felt

Cut 2 eye pieces.

Make the Superhero

Note: A short 1.5 stitch length and a ¼" (6mm) seam are used throughout.

1. Trace the required appliqué pieces from the template pages onto the paper side of the fusible webbing using a sharp pencil; leave approximately ½" (1.3cm) between each piece. You will need to trace 1 front hair piece, 2 mask pieces, the front body detail and the cape detail from the template pages. Cut the pieces out roughly, leaving ¼" (6mm) of paper around each piece.

2. Fuse the front hair piece to the orange felt, the 2 mask pieces to the black felt, the circle pieces to the white-on-white fabric and the lightning bolts to the yellow and green fabrics following the manufacturer's instructions. Cut the pieces out carefully on the lines when cool. Cut out the inner eyeholes from 1 black mask piece using a pair of small, sharp scissors.

3. Remove the backing paper from the hair piece and use the template as a guide to fuse it to the front head piece. Stitch around the hair using your favorite appliqué method (I used machine blanket stitch with matching thread). Draw the mouth on the doll then chainstitch using 2 strands of brown embroidery floss. Sew the buttons to the face for eyes using strong thread and knot securely.

4. Sew the ears together in pairs with right sides facing, leaving the bottom edge open as marked on the template. Carefully notch the seam allowances on the curves and turn the ears right-side out. Use the template as a guide to pin and then baste them to the back head piece (Figure 1).

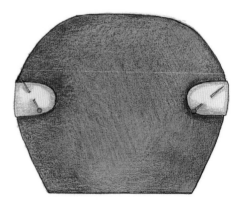

Figure 1

5. Pin and then sew the front body piece to a pants piece. Press the seam open (Figure 2).

6. Sew the 2 back body pieces together with right sides facing, leaving the seam open as marked on the template. Press the seam open. Pin and then sew a pants piece to the joined back body pieces with right sides facing. Press the seam open.

7. Press under a ¼" (6mm) hem along both long sides of the 2" × 12" (5.1cm × 30.5cm) yellow rectangle, then cut it in half across the width to give 2 pieces that measure approximately 6" (15.2cm) in length.

   Place the front of the doll right-side up on your work surface. Center and pin 1 of the yellow rectangles over the seam line between the shirt and the pants and pin it in place (Figure 3). Topstitch close to the edge down both long edges, using matching thread. Trim the edges of the belt to match the body piece. Repeat on the back of the doll (Figure 4).

8. Center the small circle (shield) and lightning bolt to the front of the doll, overlapping the belt, then fuse them in place. Stitch around the appliqué pieces as before.

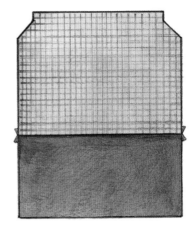

Figure 2

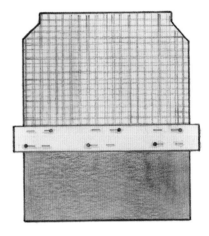

Figure 3

ALTER E8O'S

Use the Superhero body, but change up the fabrics to make a prince for the *Tiny Princesses Quilt* or a farmer to go with the *Windy Hills Farm Quilt*.

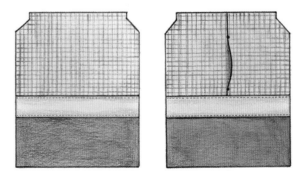

Figure 4

Figure 5

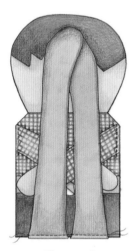

Figure 6

Figure 7

Figure 8

9. Pin and then sew the front head piece to the front of the doll with right sides facing (Figure 5). Press the seam toward the body piece. Repeat, sewing the back head piece to the back of the doll. Set them aside.

10. Sew a hand to the bottom edge of each of the arms with right sides facing. Sew the arms together in pairs with right sides facing. Leave the top and side seams open where marked on the template. Carefully notch the seam allowances on the curves and turn the arms right side out through the top opening.

11. Sew the legs together in pairs with right sides facing. Leave the top and side seams open where marked on the template. Notch the seam allowances on the curves and turn the legs right-side out through the top opening.

12. Place the front of the doll right-side up on your work surface. Use the templates as a guide to position the arms and legs right sides down and facing inward on the body. Make sure the stuffing openings are facing downward on the arms and inward on the legs. Pin and then baste them to the doll. The arms and legs are not stuffed until the doll is completed.

13. Place the front of the doll right-side up on your work surface again. Fold the arms and legs in toward the center of the body (Figure 6). Place the back of the doll on top of the front of the doll with right sides facing, taking care to tuck the ears in toward the center of the doll. Pin the shapes together well to secure. Sew around the doll using a short stitch length, being careful to catch only the basted ends of the arms, ears and legs in the seams.

14. Carefully notch the seam allowances on the curves, then gently turn the doll right-side out through the back opening. Stuff the body, arms and legs until firm. Hand-stitch the openings closed.

Make the Mask

1. Remove the backing paper from the 2 mask pieces. Place the whole mask piece on your work surface with the fusible webbing side facing up. Position the 2 white felt eye pieces on top of the mask (Figure 7), then place the remaining mask piece with the cut-out eyeholes on top, fusible webbing facing down. Use your iron to carefully fuse the mask pieces together.

2. Sew around the outside edges of the mask using matching thread and a straight stitch on your sewing machine. Stitch close to the edges. Trim any rough edges from the outside edge of the mask. Sew around the edges of the eyeholes in the same manner (Figure 8).

   Sew 2 black buttons to the white felt for eyes. Thread a large-eyed needle with the length of elasitc thread and secure the thread to each side of the mask to fit the doll.

Make the Cape

1. Center and fuse the large circle and lightning bolt to the right side of the blue cape piece, then stitch around the appliqué pieces as before (Figure 9).

2. Pin the front and the lining of the cape together with right sides facing. Use a ¼" (6mm) seam to sew around the cape, leaving the top edge open for turning. Carefully notch the seam allowances on the curves (Figure 10), and then turn the cape right-side out. Press well. Topstitch around the 3 sewn edges of the cape, stitching close to the edge, using matching thread.

3. Sew a gathering stitch along the top edge of the cape, sewing through both layers. Gently gather the cape until the gathered edge measures approximately 6½" (16.5cm) wide.

4. Iron the blue cape tie in half lengthwise with right sides facing. Find the center of the fabric strip and mark it with a pin. Measure 3¼" (8.3cm) out from each side of the center and mark with a pin (Figure 11).

5. Use a scant ¼" (6mm) seam to sew down the short edge of the tie, then along the long edge, stopping at the pin mark (Figure 12). Repeat for the opposite side. Carefully trim the corners and turn the tie right-side out. Carefully press the fabric at the opening to make a hem, then press the cape tie well.

6. Tuck the gathered edge of the cape into the opening left in the tie (Figure 13). Pin the cape in place and use small hand stitches to sew the tie to the cape on both sides. Use your sewing machine to topstitch along the tie, matching the stitches to the previously top-stitched edge. Press gently to finish.

7. Place the mask and cape on the toy to turn him from a mild-mannered doll into a crime-fighting superhero!

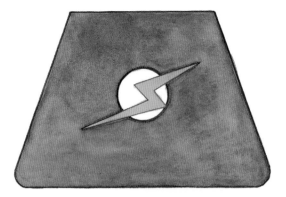

Figure 9

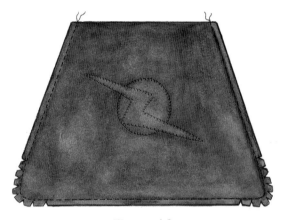

Figure 10

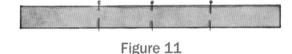

Figure 11

Figure 12

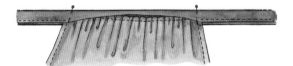

Figure 13

SNUGGLE BEARS
QUILT

Who can resist naptime with a quilt full of cuddly Snuggle Bears? This pretty quilt is easy to make and the perfect size to snuggle under. Add a sachet of lavender to the Snuggle Bear Soft Toy's stuffing for soothing dreams.

Finished Size: 55½" × 55½" (141cm × 141cm)

Materials

Background Blocks

½ yard (0.5m) each of 2 different background fabrics: pink & white small checked fabric (A) and solid medium pink fabric (B) (also used for appliqué)

⅜ yard (34cm) each of 4 different background fabrics: pink & white medium checked fabric (C); pink & white medium dot fabric (D); solid light pink fabric (E); pink-on-pink dot fabric (F) (also used for appliqué)

1 yard (0.9m) of white-on-white fabric (also used for borders and appliqué)

Borders

(1) 3½" (8.9cm) × WOF strip each of 4 different fabrics: green small floral print; lavendar small floral print; blue & white small check; yellow & white small check

Appliqué

1 yard (0.9m) total of assorted solid brown and brown-on-brown print fabrics for the bears and bees

10" × 14" (25.4cm × 35.6cm) rectangle of medium to dark brown-on-brown fabric for the noses

½ yard (0.5m) of assorted solid cream and cream print fabrics for the muzzles

12" (30.5cm) square of blue-on-blue fabric for the flower centers

12" (30.5cm) square of green & white dot fabric for the flower centers

5½" × 11" (14cm × 27.9cm) rectangle of solid yellow fabric for the flowers

3½" × 7" (8.9cm × 17.8cm) rectangle of white & purple dot fabric for the flower centers

9" (22.9cm) square of yellow-on-yellow print fabric for the beehive

6" × 9" (15.2cm × 22.9cm) of a complementary yellow-on-yellow print fabric for the beehive

Scraps of blue-on-blue, green-on-green and yellow-on-yellow fabrics for the remaining appliqué

Binding and Backing

½ yard (0.5m) of deep pink & white small dot fabric for the binding

3½ yards (3.2m) of fabric for the backing

Assorted Supplies

Light lead pencil

Fabric marking pen

Brown embroidery floss for the facial features

Matching thread to suit your favorite method of appliqué

61½" (156.2cm) square of batting

Approximately 6 yards (5.5m) of lightweight fusible web (I used Heat n Bond Lite, which measures 17" [43cm] wide)

18 pairs of assorted small buttons for the eyes

1 small pink button for the beehive

5 Snuggle Bears Quilt template pages

Cutting

Fabric A (Pink & White Small Checked)

Cut (3) 10½" (26.7cm) squares for the background blocks.

Cut (5) 5½" (14cm) squares for the background blocks.

Fabric B (Solid Medium Pink)

Cut (3) 10½" (26.7cm) squares for the background blocks.

Cut (6) 5½" (14cm) squares for the background blocks.

Fabric C (Pink & White Medium Check)

Cut (4) 10½" (26.7cm) squares for the background blocks.

Fabric D (Pink & White Medium Dot)

Cut (4) 10½" (26.7cm) squares for the background blocks.

Fabric E (Solid Light Pink)

Cut (2) 10½" (26.7cm) squares for the background blocks.

Cut (4) 5½" (26.7cm) squares for the background blocks.

Fabric F (Pink-on-Pink Dot)

Cut (3) 10½" (26.7cm) squares for the background blocks.

White-on-White Print

Cut (9) 5½" (14cm) squares for the background blocks.

Cut (3) 3" (7.6cm) × WOF strips. Subcut (39) 3" (7.6cm) squares for the border.

Border Fabrics

Cut (1) 3" (7.6cm) × WOF strip from each of the 4 fabrics. Subcut (11) 3" (7.6cm) squares from the green floral; (11) 3" (7.6cm) squares from the lavendar floral; (11) 3" (7.6cm) squares from the blue & white check; and (12) 3" (7.6cm) squares from the yellow & white check.

Binding Fabric

Cut (6) 3" (7.6cm) × WOF strips.

Backing Fabric

Cut (2) 61½" (156.2cm) lengths. Remove the selvages.

Make the Appliqué Blocks

1. Trace the required appliqué pieces from the template pages onto the paper side of the fusible webbing using a sharp pencil; leave approximately ½" (1.3cm) between each piece.

   You will need to trace the 18 bears, 2 pairs of glasses plus their lenses, 4 bows, 1 beehive, 4 bees, 6 butterflies and 18 flowers plus their centers.

2. Cut the pieces out roughly, leaving ¼" (6mm) of paper around each piece. Fuse the pieces to the fabrics you have chosen for the appliqué, following the manufacturer's instructions. Use the photo at the end of this project as your guide to color choices and placement throughout. Cut the pieces out carefully on the lines when cool.

3. Remove the backing paper from the appliqué pieces and use Figure 1 and the templates as a guide to place the bears on the 10½" (26.7cm) background blocks. The bottom raw edges of the bear's head and muzzle and the bottom raw edge of the beehive align with the bottom raw edge of the background block.

   When you are happy with the position of the appliqué pieces, fuse them to the background blocks following the manufacturer's instructions. Repeat to center and then fuse the butterflies and flowers to the (18) 5½" (14cm) background blocks. The bees aren't fused to the quilt until the center is completed.

4. Stitch around the appliqué pieces using your favorite method (I using a hand-stitched blanket stitch and 2 strands of matching embroidery floss). Use the templates as a guide to draw the mouth on each bear and the feelers on each butterfly with a fine-point fabric pen.

   Chainstitch the mouth of each bear using 2 strands of brown embroidery floss (Figure 1). Backstitch the feelers on the butterflies using 2 strands of contrasting thread. Stitch a French knot to the end of each feeler to finish (Figure 2).

Figure 1

Figure 2

63

Make the Quilt Center

1. Use Figure 3 as a guide to lay out out the finished blocks. When you are happy with the placement of the blocks, begin by sewing the flower and butterfly blocks together in pairs. Press the seams toward the darker fabric. Pin and then sew the flower/butterfly units to the bear and beehive blocks. Press the seams toward the bears. Continue to use Figure 3 as a guide to sew the blocks into 3 horizontal rows. Once each row is stitched, pin and then sew the 3 rows together, carefully matching the seams, to make the center of the quilt.

2. Use the photo at the end of this project as a guide to fuse the bees to the quilt center. Stitch around the appliqué pieces as before. Backstitch the feelers using 2 strands of contrasting embroidery floss. Stitch a French knot to the end of each feeler to finish. Press well.

Make the Borders

1. To make the side borders, sew 20 assorted 3" (7.6cm) white, green floral, purple floral, yellow check and blue checked squares together end to end. Make 2 border strips, each measuring 50½" (128.3cm) long (Figure 4). Sew a border to each side of the quilt. Press the seams outward.

2. To make the top and bottom borders, sew 22 assorted 3" (7.6cm) squares together end to end. Make 2 border strips, each measuring 55½" (141cm) long (Figure 5). Sew a border to the top and bottom of the quilt. Press the seams outward.

Prepare the Backing

1. Sew the two 61½" (156.2cm) lengths of backing fabric together along the long edges, then trim to make a piece measuring approximately 61½" (156.2cm) square.

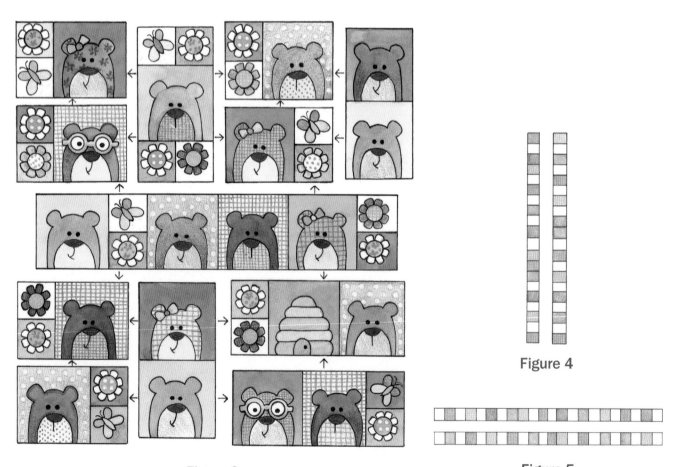

Figure 3

Figure 4

Figure 5

Finish the Quilt

1. Layer the backing, batting and quilt top (see Making a Quilt Sandwich on page 15). Baste the layers together using your favorite method. Start quilting from the center and work your way out to the edges.

2. Sew the 6 binding strips together using diagonal seams. Trim the seams to ¼" (6mm) and press them open. Fold the binding strip in half lengthwise, wrong sides facing, and press well. Sew the binding to the front of the quilt using a ½" (1.3cm) seam, and then sew the ends together where they meet. Wrap the binding to the back of the quilt and hand-stitch in place.

3. Sew buttons to the bears' faces for eyes and 1 button to the door of the beehive where indicated on the template. Sew the buttons in place through all thicknesses of the quilt using strong thread. Knot securely. Label and date your quilt to finish.

SNUGGLE BEAR
SOFT TOY

Finished Size: 17" (43.2cm) tall

Materials

⅜ yard (34cm) of brown baby corduroy for the head, arms, legs, ears and tail

12" × 14" (30.5cm × 35.6cm) rectangle of pink floral print fabric for the body

4½" × 5½" (11.4cm × 14cm) rectangle of white wool felt for the muzzle

2" × 3" (5.1cm × 7.6cm) rectangle of black wool felt for the nose

Assorted Supplies

Light lead pencil

Fabric marking pen

Black embroidery floss for the facial features

Matching thread to suit your favorite method of appliqué

8" (20.3cm) square of light-weight fusible web

2 small black buttons for the eyes

Polyester fiberfill

Tracing paper (optional)

4 *Snuggle Bear Soft Toy* template pages

TEXTURED FABRICS

The teddy bear can be made using a variety of fabrics including cotton, corduroy, denim and fleece. Adjust your sewing techniques to suit your fabric choices.

Cutting

Trace and cut out the template pieces. You will need to trace the head, front body, back body, ear, arm, leg and tail. Pin the template pieces to the fabrics you have chosen and cut the following:

Pink Floral Fabric

Cut 1 front body piece.

Cut 2 back body pieces (cut 1 in reverse).

Brown Corduroy Fabric

Cut 2 head pieces (cut 1 in reverse).

Cut 4 ear pieces (cut 2 in reverse).

Cut 4 arm pieces (cut 2 in reverse).

Cut 4 leg pieces (cut 2 in reverse).

Cut 2 tail pieces (cut 1 in reverse).

Figure 1

Figure 2

Figure 3

Make the Teddy Bear

Note: A short 1.5 stitch length and a ¼" (6mm) seam are used throughout.

1. Trace the muzzle and the nose pieces from the template pages onto the paper side of the fusible webbing using a sharp pencil; leave ½" (1.3cm) between each piece. Cut the pieces out roughly, leaving ¼" (6mm) of paper around each piece.

2. Fuse the pieces to the felt you have chosen following the manufacturer's instructions. Cut the pieces out carefully on the lines when cool. Remove the backing paper from the appliqué pieces and use the template as a guide to fuse them to the front head piece.

   Stitch around the appliqué pieces using your favorite method. (I used blanket-stitch and 2 strands of coordinating embroidery floss.) Draw the mouth on the bear and chainstitch using 2 strands of black embroidery floss. Sew 2 buttons to the face for eyes using strong thread, then knot securely (Figure 1).

3. Sew the ears together in pairs with right sides facing. Leave the bottom edge open where marked on the template. Notch the seam allowances on the curves and turn the ears right-side out through the opening. Press gently.

4. Use the template as a guide to position the ears right sides down and facing inward on the front head piece. Pin and then baste them to the face (Figure 2).

5. Pin and then sew the front head piece to the front body piece with right sides facing (Figure 3). Press the seam open and set it aside.

6. Sew the tail pieces together with right sides facing. Leave the bottom edge open as marked on the template. Notch the seam allowances on the curves and turn the tail right side out through the opening. Add a pinch of stuffing to the tail.

   Use the template as a guide to position the tail on a back body piece with the raw edges aligned. Pin then baste the tail to the back body piece (Figure 4).

7. Sew the 2 back body pieces together with right sides facing. Leave the seam open where marked on the template. Press the seam open (Figure 5).

   Pin then sew the back head piece to the joined back body pieces, right sides facing. Press the seam open.

8. Sew the arms together in pairs with right sides facing. Leave the top and side seams open where marked on the template. Notch the seam allowances on the curves and turn the arms right side out through the top opening.

   Sew the legs together in the same manner. Notch the seam allowances on the curves and turn the legs right side out through the top opening.

9. Place the front of the bear right side up on your work surface. Use the template as a guide to position the arms and legs right sides down and facing inward on the body. Make sure the stuffing openings are facing downward on the arms and inward on the legs. Pin and then baste them to the bear. The arms and legs are not stuffed until the bear is completed.

10. Place the front of the bear right side-up on your work surface again. Fold the ears, arms and legs in toward the center of the body. Place the back of the bear on top of the front of the bear with the right sides facing. Pin the shapes together well to secure. Sew around the bear using a short stitch length, being careful to catch only the basted ends of the ears, arms and legs in the seams (Figure 6). Backstitch at the beginning and end of the seam.

11. Carefully notch the seam allowance on the curves, then gently turn the bear right-side out through the back opening. Stuff the body, arms and legs until firm. Hand-stitch the openings closed.

Figure 4

Figure 5

Figure 6

HUGGABLE DURABILITY

Sew around the outside of the bear twice to strengthen and add durability to the seams.

Tiny Princesses
Quilt

Wrap yourself in royalty with this Tiny Princesses Quilt. Use the templates from the Bedtime Superheroes Quilt to add a handsome prince or two!

Finished Size: 60½" × 60½" (153.7cm × 153.7cm)

Materials

Background Blocks and Four-Patch Blocks

1 fat quarter (45.7cm × 55.9cm) of solid deep pink fabric

12½" (31.8cm) square of solid medium green fabric

⅝ yard (0.6m) each of green & white large dot, solid medium pink, green & white chevron and solid orange fabrics

⅜ yard (34cm) each of pink & orange dot, orange-on-orange striped and solid yellow fabrics

⅛ yard (11cm) total each of assorted yellow and assorted orange fabrics

¼ yard (23cm) each of solid white and pink-on-pink dot fabric

Appliqué

8" (20.3cm) square each of 16 assorted skin-colored fabrics

10" (25.4cm) square each of 16 assorted hair-colored fabrics

¼ yard (23cm) total of assorted orange solid and print fabrics

⅜ yard (34cm) total each of assorted pink, blue, yellow and white solid and print fabrics

¼ yard (23cm) total each of green, red and purple solid and print fabrics

Binding and Backing

½ yard (0.5m) of pink & white striped fabric for the binding

3¾ yards (3.4m) of fabric for the backing

Assorted Supplies

Light lead pencil

Fabric marking pen

Brown embroidery floss for the facial features

Matching thread to suit your favorite method of appliqué

66½" (168.9cm) square of batting

Approximately 7 yards (6.4m) of lightweight fusible web (I used Heat n Bond Lite, which measures 17" [43cm] wide)

16 pairs of assorted small buttons for the eyes

38 assorted jewel buttons and assorted beads for the crowns

18 *Tiny Princesses Quilt* template pages

Cutting

Solid Deep Pink Fabric
Cut (1) 12½" (31.8cm) background square.

Cut (1) 6½" (15.2cm) background square.

Green & White Large Dot Fabric
Cut (3) 12½" (31.8cm) background squares.

Cut (4) 6½" (15.2cm) background squares.

Solid Medium Pink Fabric
Cut (2) 12½" (31.8cm) background squares.

Cut (6) 6½" (15.2cm) background squares.

Green & White Chevron Fabric
Cut (2) 12½" (31.8cm) background squares.

Cut (5) 6½" (15.2cm) background squares.

Solid Medium Green Fabric
Cut (1) 12½" (31.8cm) background square.

Solid Orange Fabric
Cut (3) 12½" (31.8cm) background squares.

Cut (1) 6½" (15.2cm) background square.

Cut (2) 3½" (8.9cm) squares for the Four-Patch blocks.

Pink & Orange Dot Fabric
Cut (2) 12½" (31.8cm) background squares.

Cut (6) 3½" (8.9cm) squares for the Four-Patch blocks.

Orange-on-Orange Striped Fabric
Cut (1) 12½" (31.8cm) background square.

Cut (6) 3½" (8.9cm) squares for the Four-Patch blocks.

Solid Yellow Fabric
Cut (1) 12½" (31.8cm) background square.

Cut (1) 6½" (15.2cm) background square.

Cut (6) 3½" (8.9cm) squares for the Four-Patch blocks.

Solid White Fabric
Cut (16) 3½" (8.9cm) squares for the Four-Patch blocks.

Pink-on-Pink Dot Fabric
Cut (16) 3½" (8.9cm) squares for the Four-Patch blocks.

Assorted Yellow Fabrics
Cut (8) 3½" (8.9cm) squares for the Four-Patch blocks.

Assorted Orange Fabrics
Cut (12) 3½" (8.9cm) squares for the Four-Patch blocks.

Binding Fabric
Cut (7) 2½" (6.4cm) × WOF strips.

Backing Fabric
Cut (2) 66½" (168.9cm) lengths. Remove the selvages.

MAKE IT A TWIN

To make a twin-size quilt, add an extra row or two of princess blocks to the quilt.

Make the Appliqué Blocks

1. Trace the required appliqué pieces from the template pages onto the paper side of the fusible webbing using a sharp pencil; leave approximately ½" (1.3cm) between each piece.

   You will need to trace 16 princesses and 18 flowers plus their centers.

2. Cut the pieces out roughly, leaving ¼" (6mm) of paper around each piece. Fuse the pieces to the fabrics you have chosen for the appliqué following the manufacturer's instructions. Cut the pieces out carefully on the lines when cool.

3. Remove the backing paper from the appliqué pieces and use Figure 1 and the templates as a guide to place the princesses on the 12½" (31.8cm) background blocks. The bottom raw edges of the body and arms for each princess align with the bottom raw edge of the background block.

   When you are happy with the position of the appliqué pieces, fuse them to the background block following the manufacturer's instructions (Figure 1).

   Repeat to center and fuse the flowers to the (18) 6½" (16.5cm) background blocks (Figure 2).

4. Stitch around the appliqué pieces using your favorite method (I used hand-stitched blanket stitch and 2 strands of matching embroidery floss). Use the templates as a guide to draw the mouth on each princess using a fine-point fabric pen. Backstitch each mouth using 2 strands of brown embroidery floss.

Make the Quilt Center

1. Lay out the finished princess blocks into 4 rows, each with 4 blocks. When you are happy with the placement of the blocks, sew each horizontal row of 4 blocks together and press the seams in each row in opposite directions. Once each row is stitched, pin and then sew the 4 rows together, carefully matching the seams, to make the center of the quilt (Figure 3). Press well then set aside.

Figure 1

Figure 2

Figure 3

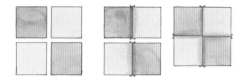

Figure 4

Figure 5   Figure 6

Make the Four-Patch Borders

1. Start with four 3½" (8.9cm) squares, 2 squares in each of 2 contrasting colors. Lay out the squares to form the block. Use a ¼" (6mm) seam to sew the squares together in pairs; then sew the pairs together to make the block (Figure 4). Press well. Repeat to make 18 Four-Patch blocks.

2. To make the side borders, sew 4 Four-Patch blocks and 4 flower blocks together end to end, alternating the blocks as you sew. Make 2 borders each measuring 48½" (123.2cm) long (Figure 5). Sew 1 of these to each side of the quilt. Press the seams outward.

3. To make the top and bottom borders, sew 5 Four-Patch blocks and 5 flower blocks together end to end, alternating the blocks as you sew. Make 2 strips each measuring 60½" (157.3cm) long (Figure 6). Sew these to the top and bottom of the quilt. Press the seams outward.

Prepare the Backing

1. Sew the two 66½" (168.9cm) lengths of backing fabric together along the long edges. Trim to make a piece approximately 66½"(168.9cm) square.

Finishing

1. Layer the backing, batting and quilt top (see Making a Quilt Sandwich on page 15). Baste the layers together using your favorite method. Start quilting from the center and work your way out to the edges.

2. Sew the 7 binding strips together using straight seams to preserve the striped pattern. Press the seams open. Fold the binding strip in half lengthwise, wrong sides facing, and press well. Sew the binding to the front of the quilt using a ¼" (6mm) seam, and then sew the ends together where they meet. Wrap the binding to the back of the quilt and hand-stitch in place.

3. Sew buttons to the princesses' faces for eyes and the jewel buttons to their crowns where indicated on the pattern template. Sew the buttons in place through all thicknesses of the quilt using strong thread. Knot securely. Label and date your quilt to finish.

MAKE THEM SPARKLE

Have lots of fun adding sparkling bling
to the princesses' crowns and dresses.

Tiny Princess
SOFT TOY

Finished Size: 20" (50.8cm) tall

Materials

Princess with Braided Hair

8" × 15" (20.3cm × 38.1cm) rectangle of skin-colored wool felt for the face and hands

12" (30.5cm) square of bright pink wool felt for the hair and shoes

12" (30.5cm) square of bright orange wool felt for the hair

8" (20.3cm) square of bright golden yellow wool felt for the crown

8" × 16" (20.3cm × 40.6cm) rectangle of purple & white floral fabric for the body

9" (22.9cm) square of complementary floral print fabric for the arms

7" × 12" (17.8cm × 30.5cm) rectangle of gray & white striped fabric for the legs

2" × 5" (5.1cm × 12.7cm) rectangle of white-on-white fabric for the collar

2" × 10" (5.1cm × 25.4cm) rectangle of solid yellow fabric for the crown

Princess with Pigtails

Use the materials list for the Princess with Braided Hair and the photograph of the Princess with Pigtails to choose your fabrics

You will need a 16" (40.6cm) square of wool felt for the hair and a 9" (22.9cm) square of yellow wool felt for the shoes

Assorted Supplies

Light lead pencil

Fabric marking pen

Brown embroidery floss for the facial features

Matching thread to suit your favorite method of appliqué

Approximately ¼ yard (23cm) of lightweight fusible web (I used Heat n Bond Lite, which measures 17" [43cm] wide)

2 small brown buttons for the eyes

20" (50.8cm) piece of ¼" (6mm) wide elastic for the crown

1 large jewel button for the dress

3 small jewel buttons for the crown

Polyester fiberfill

Tracing paper (optional)

5 *Tiny Princess Soft Toy* template pages

Skirt (optional)

¼ yard (23cm) of solid white fabric

¼ yard (23cm) white & silver dot tulle

1½" × 11½" (3.8cm × 29.2cm) piece of lightweight interfacing

3 snap closures

3 small white pearl buttons

Cutting for the Princess with Braids

Trace and cut out the template pieces. You will need to trace the head, front body, back body, arm, hand, leg, shoe and crown pieces. Pin the template pieces to the fabrics you have chosen and cut the following:

Purple & White Floral Fabric

Cut 1 front body piece.

Cut 2 back body pieces (cut 1 in reverse).

Complementary Floral Fabric

Cut 4 arm pieces (cut 2 in reverse).

Gray & White Stripe Fabric

Cut 4 leg pieces (cut 2 in reverse).

Skin-Colored Felt

Cut 1 head piece.

Cut 4 hand pieces (cut 2 in reverse).

Orange Felt

Cut 1 head piece in reverse.

Cut (1) 4" × 9" (10.2cm × 22.9cm) rectangle for the braids.

Pink Felt

Cut 4 shoe pieces (cut 2 in reverse).

Cut (1) 3" × 9" (7.6cm × 22.9cm) rectangle for the braids.

Solid Yellow Fabric

Cut (1) 1½" × 8½" (3.8cm × 21.6cm) rectangle for the crown.

Solid White Fabric (optional)

Cut (1) 8½" × 26½" (21.6cm × 67.3cm) rectangle for the skirt.

Cut (2) 1½" × 11½" (3.8cm × 29.2cm) rectangles for the waistband.

Lightweight Interfacing (optional)

Cut (1) 1½" × 11½" (3.8cm × 29.2cm) rectangle for the waistband.

White & Silver Tulle (optional)

Cut (1) 8½" × 36½" (21.6cm × 92.7cm) rectangle for the skirt.

Figure 1

Make the Princess

Note: A short 1.5 stitch length and a ¼" (6mm) seam are used throughout.

1. Trace 1 front hair piece, 1 collar piece and 2 crown pieces from the template pages onto the paper side of the fusible webbing using a sharp pencil; leave ½" (1.3cm) between each piece. Cut the pieces out roughly, leaving ¼" (6mm) of paper around each piece.

2. Fuse the front hair piece to the orange felt, the collar piece to the white-on-white fabric and the crown pieces to the yellow felt following the manufacturer's instructions. Cut the pieces out carefully on the lines when cool. Set the 2 crown pieces aside.

3. Remove the backing paper from the remaining appliqué pieces and use the template as a guide to fuse the hair to the front head piece and the collar to the top of the front body piece.

78

4. Stitch around the appliqué pieces using your favorite method (I used hand-stitched blanket-stitch and 2 strands of matching embroidery floss). Draw the mouth on the doll and chainstitch using 2 strands of brown embroidery floss. Sew the buttons to the face for eyes and the jewel button to the collar using strong thread. Knot securely (Figure 1).

5. Pin and then sew the front head piece to the front body piece with right sides facing (Figure 2). Press the seam open. Set it aside.

6. Sew the 2 back body pieces together with right sides facing. Leave the seam open where marked on the template. Press the seam open. Pin and then sew the back head piece to the joined back body pieces with right sides facing.

7. Take the orange and pink felt you are using for the braids and stitch 4 rectangles measuring approximately ½" × 8½" (1.3cm × 21.6cm) directly onto the orange felt, and 2 rectangles measuring ½" × 8½" (1.3cm × 21.6cm) onto the pink felt, leaving ¼" (6mm) between them. Cut the braids out, cutting close to the stitching line (Figure 3).

8. Place 2 orange braid strips and 1 pink braid strip on top of each other. Use the template as a guide to position the braids on the right side of the back head piece. Leave approximately ¼" (6mm) overhang on the braids. Pin and then baste the braids in place. The braids will face inward. Repeat to baste the second braid strips to the opposite side of the back head piece (Figure 4).

Figure 2

Figure 3

Figure 4

FOR THE PRINCESS WITH PIGTAILS

If you are making the doll with pigtails, trace and cut out 1 pigtail pattern piece. Pin the template piece to the black felt and cut out 4 pigtail pieces (cut 2 in reverse). Sew the pigtail pieces together in pairs with right sides facing. Notch the seam allowances on the curves and turn them right-side out. Stuff lightly. Follow the instructions for the doll, replacing the braids with the pigtails.

Figure 5

Figure 6

Figure 7

Figure 8

9. Sew a hand to the bottom edge of each arm with right sides facing (Figure 5).

   Pin and then sew the arms together in pairs with right sides facing. Leave the top and side seams open where marked on the template. Notch the seam allowances on the curves and turn the arms right side out through the top opening.

10. Sew the shoes to the legs, then sew the legs together in the same way as the arms. Notch the seam allowances on the curves, then turn the legs right-side out through the top opening. (Figure 6).

11. Place the front of the doll right-side up on your work surface. Use the template as a guide to position the arms and legs right sides down and facing inward on the body. Make sure the stuffing openings are facing downward on the arms and inward on the legs. Pin and then baste them to the doll. The arms and legs are not stuffed until the doll is completed (Figure 7).

12. Place the front of the doll right-side up on your work surface again. Fold the arms and legs in toward the center of the body. Place the back of the doll on top of the front of the doll with right sides facing, taking care to tuck the braids in toward the center of the doll. Pin the shapes together well to secure.

    Sew around the doll using a short stitch length, being careful to only catch the basted ends of the braids, arms and legs in the seams. (Use your fingers to feel where the arms, legs and braids are situated, and gently push them aside if they are in the way of the seam.)

13. Carefully notch the seam allowances on the curves, then gently turn the doll right-side out through the back opening. Stuff the body, arms and legs until firm. Hand-stitch the openings closed.

14. Braid the three strands of felt hair. Use matching thread and tiny stitches to secure the ends of the braids in place (Figure 8).

Make the Crown

1. Iron the yellow rectangle in half lengthwise with right sides facing. Sew a scant ¼" (6mm) seam down the long length, then turn the casing right-side out and press. Thread the elastic through the casing and pin it in place at each end (Figure 9). Secure the elastic in place with a few hand-stitches.

2. Place the 2 crown pieces together, the sides with the fusible webbing facing each other. Tuck the ends of the elastic casing between the 2 pieces on the left- and right-hand bottom edges, and pin them in place (Figure 10). Check to see if the crown fits the doll's head and adjust as necessary. Use the tip of the iron to carefully fuse the crown pieces together. Don't remove the pins holding the elastic casing.

3. Sew around the outside edges of the crown 2 or 3 times using matching thread. Stitch close to the edges, catching the elastic casing in the seam. Trim any rough edges from the crown and sew 3 jewel buttons to the crown using strong thread to finish (Figure 11).

Figure 9

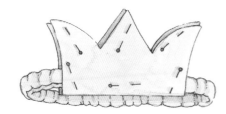

Figure 10

Figure 11

Make the Skirt

1. Iron the interfacing to the wrong side of 1 solid white waistband piece. Refer to the skirt illustrations for Penny the Pig throughout.

2. Sew a double ¼" (6mm) hem on both short sides and 1 long side of the solid white skirt piece. Topstitch along each edge.

3. Gather the top edge of the solid white skirt piece until it fits the long edge of the waistband leaving ¼" (6mm) of waistband at each end. Gather the top edge of the tulle piece to the same width. Smooth out the gathers on both pieces evenly as you go. Baste the 2 skirt pieces together along the top gathered edge.

4. Carefully pin and then sew the gathered skirt to 1 long edge of the interfaced-waistband piece, with right sides facing. Remove the gathering stitch/thread, then gently press the seam toward the waistband.

5. Press under a ¼" (6mm) hem on 1 long edge of the remaining waistband piece. Pin and then sew the hemmed waistband to the waistband on the skirt, right sides together.

Start sewing at the hemline on 1 short edge, sewing across the top, then down the opposite short edge, stopping again at the hemmed edge.

6. Trim the corners and turn the waistband right-side out; press. Tuck the gathered skirt seam under the waistband and pin it in place. Slipstitch the waistband to the skirt, covering the gathered edge as you sew.

7. Topstitch along the top and bottom edges of the waistband, stitching close to the top edge and the seam between the waistband and the skirt. Press carefully, so as not to melt the tulle with the iron. If the bottom edge of the tulle is longer than the white underskirt, neatly trim the tulle to match.

8. Sew 3 snaps to the skirt, starting at the waistband and placing them evenly down the back opening. Sew 3 decorative buttons to the right side of the skirt opening. Place the skirt on the princess to finish.

WINDY HILL FARM
QUILT

Welcome to Windy Hill, where the sun is always shining and the air is always sweet. A border of pretty pinwheels ensures that this quilt will brighten any room. Penny the Pig, a resident of Windy Hill Farm, is waiting to become your best friend!

Finished Size: 60½" × 72½" (153.7cm × 184.2cm)

Materials

Background and Pinwheel blocks

¾ yard (0.7m) each of solid yellow, solid green and solid light blue fabrics

½ yard (0.5m) each of solid medium blue and solid medium orange fabric

⅜ yard (34cm) total of assorted light blue-on-blue print fabric

⅛ yard (11cm) each of blue & white dot, pink-on-pink dot and pink & white checked fabrics

⅞ yard (0.8m) solid light cream fabric

¼ yard (23cm) total of assorted light yellow-on-yellow print fabrics

Appliqué

⅜ yard (34cm) total each of assorted pink, black and orange solid and print fabrics

¾ yard (0.7m) total of assorted brown solid and print fabrics

½ yard (0.5m) total of assorted white-on-white print fabrics

¼ yard (23cm) total each of assorted black & white dot fabrics and cream-on-cream fabrics

6" (15.2cm) × WOF total of assorted red print fabrics

1 fat eighth (45.7cm × 27.9cm) each of solid gray-brown fabric and solid yellow fabric

12" (30.5cm) square each of solid purple fabric, skin-colored fabric and denim blue fabric

5" × 10½" (12.7cm × 26.7cm) rectangle each of red & white small checked fabric and blue & white dot fabric for the farmers' shirts

8" (20.3cm) square of yellow & white dot fabric for the sun

Scraps of solid dark green fabric for the flower stem and leaves

Binding and Backing

½ yard (0.5m) of light blue fabric for the binding

4⅜ yards (4.4m) of fabric for the backing

Assorted Supplies

Light lead pencil

Fabric marking pen

Brown, black and white embroidery floss for the facial features

Matching thread to suit your favorite method of appliqué

66½" × 78½" (168.9cm × 199.4cm) piece of batting

Approximately 7 yards (6.4m) of lightweight fusible web (I used Heat n Bond Lite, which measures 17" [43cm] wide)

23 pairs of assorted small buttons for the eyes

2 medium yellow buttons for the overalls

2 medium white buttons for the overalls

4 small and 4 tiny pink buttons for the pigs' snouts

36 *Windy Hill Farm Quilt* template pages

Cutting

Solid Yellow Fabric

Cut (2) 12½" (31.8cm) × WOF strips. Subcut (3) 12½" (31.8cm) squares and (1) 12½" × 18½" (31.8cm × 47cm) rectangle for the background blocks.

Cut (6) 3⅞" (9.8cm) squares. Cut each square once on the diagonal to yield 12 half-square triangles for the Pinwheel blocks.

Solid Medium Orange Fabric

Cut (1) 12½" (31.8cm) × WOF strip. Subcut (2) 12½" (31.8cm) squares for the background blocks.

Cut (1) 3⅞" (9.8cm) × WOF strip. Subcut (8) 3⅞" (9.8cm) squares. Cut across each square on the diagonal to yield 16 half-square triangles for the Pinwheel blocks.

From the remaining fabric, cut (12) 3⅞" (9.8cm) squares. Cut across each square on the diagonal to yield 24 half-square triangles for the Pinwheel blocks.

Solid Green Fabric

Cut (2) 12½" (31.8cm) × WOF strips. Subcut (1) 12½" (31.8cm) square and (2) 12½" × 18½" (31.8cm × 47cm) rectangles for the background blocks.

Cut (16) 3⅞" (9.8cm) squares. Cut across each square on the diagonal to yield 32 half-square triangles for the Pinwheel blocks.

Solid Light Blue Fabric

Cut (2) 12½" (31.8cm) × WOF strips. Subcut (2) 12½" (31.8cm) squares and (1) 12½" × 18½" (31.8cm × 47cm) rectangle for the background blocks.

Cut (10) 3⅞" (9.8cm) squares. Cut across each square on the diagonal to yield 20 half-square triangles for the Pinwheel blocks.

Solid Medium Blue Fabric

Cut (1) 12½" (31.8cm) × WOF strip. Subcut (3) 12½" (31.8cm) squares for the background blocks.

Cut (1) 3⅞" (9.8cm) × WOF strips. Subcut (6) 3⅞" (9.8cm) squares. Cut across each square on the diagonal to yield 12 half-square triangles for the Pinwheel blocks.

Blue & White Dot Fabric

Cut (1) 3⅞" (9.8cm) × WOF strips. Subcut (8) 3⅞" (9.8cm) squares. Cut across each square on the diagonal to yield 16 half-square triangles for the Pinwheel blocks.

Solid Light Cream Fabric

Cut (1) 12½" (31.8cm) × WOF strip. Subcut (3) 12½" (31.8cm) squares for the background blocks.

Cut (4) 3⅞" (9.8cm) × WOF strips. Subcut (38) 3⅞" (9.8cm) squares. Cut across each square on the diagonal to yield 76 half-square triangles for the Pinwheel blocks.

Pink-on-Pink Dot Fabric

Cut (1) 3⅞" (9.8cm) × WOF strips. Subcut (6) 3⅞" (9.8cm) squares. Cut across each square on the diagonal to yield 12 half-square triangles for the Pinwheel blocks.

Pink & White Small Checked Fabric

Cut (1) 3⅞" (9.8cm) × WOF strips. Subcut (8) 3⅞" (9.8cm) squares. Cut across each square on the diagonal to yield 16 half-square triangles for the Pinwheel blocks.

Light Yellow-on-Yellow Print Fabrics

Cut (18) 3⅞" (9.8cm) squares. You will need to cut 2 matching squares per block. Cut across each square on the diagonal to give 4 half-square triangles for each Pinwheel block (a total of 36).

Light Blue-on-Blue Print Fabrics

Cut (24) 3⅞" (9.8cm) squares. You will need to cut 2 matching squares per block. Cut across each square on the diagonal to give 4 half-square triangles for each Pinwheel block (a total of 48).

Binding Fabric

Cut (7) 2½" (6.4cm) × WOF strips.

Backing Fabric

Cut (2) 78½" (199.4cm) lengths. Remove the selvages.

Make the Appliqué Blocks

1. Trace the required appliqué pieces from the template pages onto the paper side of the fusible webbing using a sharp pencil; leave approximately ½" (1.3cm) between each piece.

   You will need to trace 5 chickens, 2 ducks, 2 horses, 2 sheep, 2 cows, 2 large pigs, 2 small pigs, 2 goats, 1 cat, 1 dog, 5 flowers, 1 sun, 1 boy farmer and 1 girl farmer.

2. Cut the pieces out roughly, leaving ¼" (6mm) of paper around each piece. Fuse the pieces to the fabrics you have chosen for the appliqué following the manufacturer's instructions. Cut the pieces out carefully on the lines when cool.

3. Remove the backing paper from the appliqué pieces and use Figure 1 and the templates as a guide to place the pieces on the background blocks. The bottom raw edges of the appliqué pieces align with the bottom raw edges of the background blocks.

   When you are happy with the position of the appliqué pieces, fuse them to the background blocks following the manufacturer's instructions. The small pigs and the 3 flowers in Rows 1, 3 and 5 aren't fused to the quilt until the center section is completed.

4. Stitch around the appliqué pieces using your favorite method (I used a machine blanket stitch). Use the templates as a guide to draw the features on each animal or farmer using a fine-point fabric pen. Backstitch the features using 2 strands of contrasting thread.

Figure 1

Make the Quilt Center

1. Use Figure 2 as a guide to lay out the finished farmyard blocks in 5 rows. Three rows have four 12½" (31.8cm) blocks and 2 rows have one 12½" (31.8cm) and two 12½" × 18½" (31.8cm × 47cm) blocks. When you are happy with the placement of the blocks, sew each horizontal row of blocks together and press the seams in each row in opposite directions.

2. Use Figure 2 as a guide to fuse the 3 flowers and 2 small pigs to the rows 1, 3 and 5, overlapping the seams where necessary. Stitch around the appliqué pieces as before.

3. Pin and then sew the 5 rows together, carefully matching the seams, to make the center of the quilt. Press well then set aside.

Figure 2

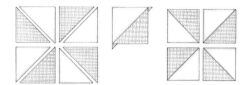

Figure 3

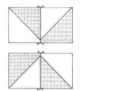

Figure 4   Figure 5

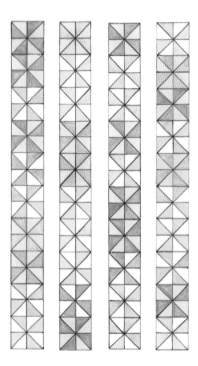

Figure 6

ADJUST THE BORDERS

The length of the borders can be adjusted as needed by stitching random seams along the border wider or narrower.

Make the Borders

1. Use the photo at the end of this project as a guide to sort the 3⅞" (9.8cm) half-square triangles into 40 groups of 8. Each group is made up of 4 matching triangles in each of 2 different fabrics. You will need to make 8 green-and-white blocks, 6 orange-and-yellow blocks, 7 pink-and-white blocks, 12 blue-and-light blue blocks, 4 orange-and-white blocks, and 3 yellow-and-light yellow blocks.

2. Choose a group of 8 triangles and lay them out on your work surface in the shape of the Pinwheel block. Sew the triangles together in pairs along the bias edges using ¼" (6mm) seams to make 4 squares. Press the seams toward the darker fabric (Figure 3).

3. Sew the squares together into pairs (Figure 4). Press the seams in opposite directions so they will lay flat when the block is finished.

   Sew the 2 units together to finish the block (Figure 5). Press the seam to 1 side. Repeat to make 40 Pinwheel blocks.

4. To make the borders, sew 10 Pinwheel blocks together end to end, carefully matching the seams. Make 4 borders each measuring 60½" (153.7cm) long (Figure 6). Sew a border to each side of the quilt. Sew the remaining borders to the top and bottom of the quilt. Press the seams outward.

Prepare the Backing

1. Sew the two 78½" (199.4cm) lengths of backing fabric together along the long edges, then trim to make a piece measuring approximately 66½" × 78½" (168.9cm × 199.4cm).

Finish the Quilt

1. Layer the backing, batting and quilt top (see Making a Quilt Sandwich on page 15). Baste the layers together using your favorite method. Start quilting from the center and work your way out to the edges.

2. Sew the 7 binding strips together using diagonal seams. Trim the seams to ¼" (6mm) and press them open. Fold the binding strip in half lengthwise, wrong sides facing, and press well. Sew the binding to the front of the quilt using a ¼" (6mm) seam, and then sew the ends together where they meet. Wrap the binding to the back and hand-stitch in place.

3. Sew buttons to all the faces and overalls where indicated on the templates. Sew the buttons in place through all thicknesses of the quilt using strong thread. Knot securely. Label and date your quilt to finish.

PENNY THE PIG

SOFT TOY

Finished Size: 16" (40.6cm) tall

Materials

⅜ yard (34cm) of solid light pink felt for the head, arms, legs and tail

8" (20.3cm) square of matching solid light pink fabric for the ears

4" × 15" (10.2cm × 38.1cm) rectangle of red-on-red dot fabric for the body

1½" × 15" (3.8cm × 38.1cm) strip of gray & white striped fabric for the body

3" × 15" (7.6m × 38.1cm) rectangle of white & orange checked fabric for the body

4" × 9" (10.2cm × 22.9cm) rectangle of pink floral fabric for the ears

6½" (16.5) × WOF of red & multi-colored dot fabric for the skirt

3" × 3½" (7.6cm × 8.9cm) rectangle of light pink-on-pink fabric for the nose

Scrap of white-on-white fabric for the shirt detail

Assorted Supplies

Light lead pencil

Fabric marking pen

Brown embroidery floss for the facial features

Matching thread to suit your favorite method of appliqué

Scrap of lightweight fusible web

1½" × 11½" (3.8cm × 29.2cm) strip of lightweight interfacing for the skirt

3 snaps for the skirt

3 small pearl/white buttons for the skirt

2 small black buttons for the eyes

2 small blue buttons for the shirt

2 small pink buttons for the nose (optional)

6" (15.2cm) piece of ½" (1.3m) wide elastic

Polyester fiberfill

Tracing paper (optional)

4 *Penny the Pig Soft Toy* template pages

89

Cutting

Trace and cut out the template pieces. You will need to trace the head, ear, front body, back body, arm and leg pieces. Pin the template pieces to the fabrics you have chosen and cut the following:

White & Orange Checked Fabric

Cut (1) 3" × 15" (7.6cm × 38.1cm) rectangle for the body.

Gray & White Striped Fabric

Cut (1) 1½" × 15" (3.8cm × 38.1cm) rectangle for the body.

Red-on-Red Dot Fabric

Cut (1) 4" × 15" (10.2cm × 38.1cm) rectangle for the body.

Solid Pink Fabric

Cut (2) 1¼" × 6" (3.2cm × 15.2cm) rectangles for the tail.

Cut 2 ear pieces (cut 1 in reverse).

Solid Pink Felt

Cut 2 head pieces (cut 1 in reverse).

Cut 4 arm pieces (cut 2 in reverse).

Cut 4 leg pieces (cut 2 in reverse).

Pink Floral Print Fabric

Cut 2 ear pieces (cut 1 in reverse).

Red & Multi-Dot Fabric

Cut (1) 6½" × 26½" (16.5cm × 67.3cm) rectangle for the skirt.

Cut (2) 1½" × 11½" (3.8cm × 29.2cm) strips for the waistband.

Interfacing

Cut (1) 1½" × 11½" (3.8cm × 29.2cm) strip for the waistband

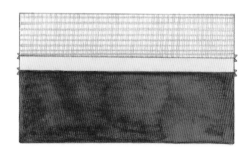

Figure 1

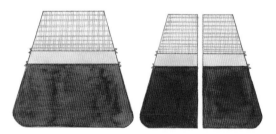

Figure 2

Make the Pig

Note: A short 1.5 stitch length and a ¼" (6mm) seam are used throughout.

1. Sew the white & orange checked rectangle, the gray & white striped rectangle and the red-on-red dot rectangle together along the long edges. (Figure 1). Press the seam open.

2. Pin the front and back body template pieces to the completed fabric unit, aligning the top edges of the template and the white & orange checked fabric. Cut 1 front body piece and 2 back body pieces from the fabric, remembering to cut 1 back body piece in reverse (Figure 2).

3. Trace the nose and shirt pieces from the template page onto the paper side of the fusible webbing using a sharp pencil; leave ½" (1.3cm) between each piece.

Cut the pieces out roughly, leaving ¼" (6mm) of paper around each piece.

4. Fuse the nose to the pink-on-pink print fabric and the shirt detail to the white-on-white fabric following the manufacturer's instructions. Cut the pieces out carefully on the lines when cool. Remove the backing paper from the nose and use the template as a guide to fuse it to the front head piece. Repeat to fuse the shirt detail to the front body piece.

5. Stitch around the nose and shirt detail using your favorite appliqué method. (I used machine blanket stitch and matching thread.) Sew the black buttons to the face for eyes and the pink buttons to the nose (optional) using strong thread and knot securely. Draw the mouth on the pig and backstitch using 2 strands of brown embroidery floss.

6. Pin and then sew the front head piece to the front body piece with right sides facing. Press the seam downward. Sew 2 blue buttons to the front shirt detail using strong thread and knot securely (Figure 3). Set this aside.

7. Sew the ears together in pairs, a solid pink ear to a pink floral print ear with right sides facing. Leave the bottom edge open where marked on the template. Notch the seam allowances on the curves and turn the ears right-side out through the opening. Press gently. Make 2 small pleats in the center of each ear and baste the pleats in place.

8. Use the template as a guide to position the ears, solid pink sides down and facing inward, on the back head piece. Pin and then baste them in place (Figure 4).

9. Place the two 1¼" × 6" (3.2cm × 15.2cm) solid pink rectangles together with right sides facing, and stitch around 3 sides, leaving 1 short end open. Place the 6" (15.2cm) piece of elastic on top, centering the raw edge of the elastic on the sewn short end of the fabric, and stitch it securely in place. Turn the tail right-side out, then pull the fabric up to expose the elastic to make a wiggly tail that measures approximately 2½" (6.4cm) in length. Pin the elastic in place, then trim the elastic to fit the tail (Figure 5). Secure the elastic in place with a few hand stitches.

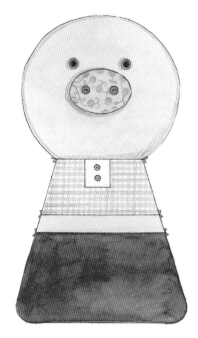

Figure 3

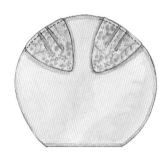

Figure 4

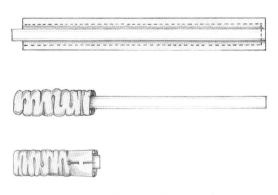

Figure 5

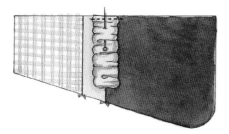

Figure 6

Figure 7

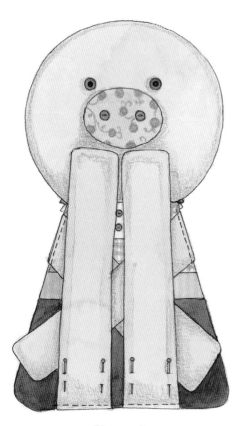

Figure 8

10. Use the template as a guide to position the tail on 1 of the back body pieces. Leave approximately ¼" (6mm) overhang on the tail. Pin and then baste the tail to the back body piece (Figure 6).

11. Sew the 2 back body pieces together with right sides facing. Leave the seam open where marked on the template (Figure 7). Press the seam open.

    Pin and then sew the back head piece to the joined back body pieces with right sides facing. Press the seam downward.

12. Sew the arms together in pairs with right sides facing. Leave the top and side seams open where marked on the template. Notch the seam allowances on the curves and turn the arms right-side out through the top opening.

13. Sew the legs together in the same manner. Notch the seam allowances on the curves and turn the legs right side out through the top opening.

14. Place the front of the pig right side up on your work surface. Use the template as a guide to position the arms and legs right sides down and facing inward on the body. Make sure the stuffing openings are facing downward on the arms and inward on the legs. Pin and then baste them to the pig (Figure 8). The arms and legs are not stuffed until the pig is completed.

15. Place the front of the pig right-side up on your work surface again. Fold the arms and legs in toward the center of the body. Place the back of the pig on top of the front of the pig with right sides facing. Take care to tuck the ears in toward the center of the pig. Pin the shapes together well to secure. Sew around the pig using a short stitch length, being careful to catch only the basted ends of the ears, arms and legs in the seams.

16. Carefully notch the seam allowance on the curves, then gently turn the pig right-side out through the back opening. Stuff the body, arms and legs until firm. Hand-stitch the openings closed. Fold the ears over and stitch them in place using tiny hand stitches and matching thread.

Make the Skirt

1. Iron the interfacing to the wrong side of a red & multi-dot waistband piece.

2. Sew a double ¼" (6mm) hem on both short sides and 1 long side of the red skirt piece (Figure 9). Top-stitch along each edge.

3. Gather the top edge of the skirt until it fits the long edge of the waistband leaving ¼" (6mm) of waistband at each end; smooth out the gathers evenly as you go. Pin and then sew the gathered skirt to 1 long edge of the interfaced-waistband with right sides facing (Figure 10). Remove the gathering stitch, then gently press the seams toward the waistband.

4. Press under a ¼" (6mm) hem on 1 long edge of the remaining waistband piece. Pin and then sew the hemmed waistband to the waistband on the skirt, right sides together.

    Start sewing at the hemline on 1 short edge, sewing across the top, then down the opposite short edge, stopping again at the hemmed edge (Figure 11).

5. Trim the corners and turn the waistband right-side out; press. Tuck the gathered skirt seam under the waistband and pin it in place. Slipstitch the waistband to the skirt, covering the gathered edge as you sew (Figure 12).

6. Topstitch along the top and bottom edges of the waistband, stitching close to the top edge and the seam between the waistband and the skirt, then press. Backstitch at the beginning and end of the seams.

7. Sew 3 snaps to the skirt, starting at the waistband and placing them evenly down the opening. Sew three decorative buttons to the right side of the skirt opening. Place the skirt on the pig to finish.

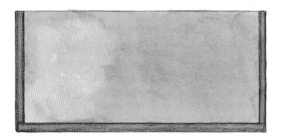

Figure 9

Figure 10

Figure 11

Figure 12

SPEEDY RACERS
QUILT

The cars are at the starting line, ready to race! Four-Patch blocks combine with appliqué stars and speedy cars for a winning quilt. The Speedy Racer Soft Toy is quick to make, so he can join you on the track in no time!

Finished Size: 57½" × 60½" (146.1cm × 153.7cm)

Materials

Background Blocks and Borders

⅞ yard (0.8m) of solid red fabric

½ yard (0.5m) each of natural linen, solid orange and corn-flower blue fabric

¾ yard (0.7m) of black & white medium checked fabric (also for binding)

⅜ yard (34cm) of solid light blue fabric (also for borders)

5½" (14cm) square of solid dark orange fabric

12" (30.5cm) square of solid light yellow fabric

⅝ yard (0.6m) of solid white fabric (also for appliqué)

12" (30.5cm) square of solid light green fabric

Four-Patch Blocks and Appliqué

10" (24.5cm) square each of 4 different fabrics: orange & white dot, red & white dot, solid medium green and blue & white dot fabric

¼ yard (23cm) total each of assorted fabrics in green, red, yellow and black & white

½ yard (0.5m) total of assorted blue fabrics

Scraps of assorted orange and purple fabrics

¼ yard (23cm) of solid black fabric

Backing

3¾ yards (3.4m) of fabric

Assorted Supplies

Light lead pencil

Fabric marking pen

Matching thread to suit your favorite method of appliqué

63½" × 66½" (161.3cm × 168.9cm) piece of batting

Approximately 6 yards (5.5cm) of lightweight fusible web (I used Heat n Bond Lite, which measures 17" [43cm] wide)

8 *Speedy Racers Quilt* template pages

Cutting

Solid Red Fabric

Cut (1) 16½" (41.9cm) × WOF strip. Subcut (3) 10½" × 16½" (26.7cm × 41.9cm) rectangles for the background blocks.

Cut (2) 5½" (14cm) × WOF strips. Subcut (2) 5½" (14cm) squares for the background blocks; and (1) 5½" × 10½" (14cm × 26.7cm) rectangle, (2) 5½" × 16½" (14cm × 41.9cm) rectangles and (1) 5½" × 20½" (14cm × 52.1cm) rectangle for the border.

Solid Linen Fabric

Cut (1) 16½" (41.9cm) × WOF strip. Subcut (3) 10½" × 16½" (26.7cm × 41.9cm) rectangles for the background blocks.

Cut (3) 5½" (14cm) squares for the background blocks.

Sold Orange Fabric

Cut (1) 16½" (41.9cm) × WOF strip. Subcut (2) 5½" × 16½" (14cm × 41.9cm) rectangles, then trim 1 rectangle to measure 5½" × 15½" (14cm × 39.4cm) for the border.

Cut (2) 10½" × 16½" (26.7cm × 41.9cm) rectangles and (2) 5½" (14cm) squares for the background blocks.

Solid Cornflower Blue Fabric

Cut (1) 16½" (41.9cm) × WOF strip. Subcut (1) 5½" × 16½" (14cm × 41.9cm) rectangle for the border. Then trim to 5½" × 15½" (14cm × 39.4cm).

Cut (2) 10½" × 16½" (26.7cm × 41.9cm) rectangles and (4) 5½" (14cm) squares for the background blocks.

Black & White Checked Fabric

Cut (2) 5½" (14cm) × WOF strips. Subcut (8) 5½" (14cm) squares for the background blocks.

Cut (6) 2½" (6.4m) × WOF strips for the binding.

Solid Light Blue Fabric

Cut (2) 5½" (14cm) × WOF strips. Subcut (4) 5½" (14cm) squares for the background blocks; and (1) 5½" × 10½" (14cm × 26.7cm) rectangle and

(1) 5½" × 16½" (14cm × 41.9cm) rectangle for the borders.

Solid Dark Orange Fabric

Cut (1) 5½" (14cm) square.

Solid Light Yellow Fabric

Cut (4) 5½" (14cm) squares.

Solid White Fabric

Cut (2) 3" (7.6cm) × WOF strips. Subcut (24) 3" (7.6cm) squares for the Four-Patch blocks.

Cut (3) 5½" (14cm) squares from the remaining fabric.

Solid Light Green Fabric

Cut (3) 5½" (14cm) squares for the background blocks.

Solid Medium Green Fabric

Cut (6) 3" (7.6cm) squares for the Four-Patch blocks.

Orange & White Dot fabric

Cut (8) 3" (7.6cm) squares for the Four-Patch blocks.

Blue & White Dot Fabric

Cut (4) 3" (7.6cm) squares for the Four-Patch blocks.

Red & White Dot Fabric

Cut (6) 3" (7.6cm) squares for the Four-Patch blocks.

Backing Fabric

Cut (2) 66½" (168.9cm) lengths. Remove the selvages.

ADD EXTRA CARS

To make this quilt for a twin-size bed, add an extra row or two of car blocks.

Make the Appliqué Blocks

1. Trace the required appliqué pieces from the template pages onto the paper side of the fusible webbing using a sharp pencil; leave approximately ½" (1.3cm) between each piece. You will need to trace 6 of Car A, 4 of Car B and 16 stars.

2. Cut the pieces out roughly, leaving ¼" (6mm) of paper around each piece. Fuse the pieces to the fabrics you have chosen for the appliqué, following the manufacturer's instructions. Cut the pieces out carefully on the lines when cool.

3. Remove the backing paper from the appliqué pieces. Use Figure 1 and the templates as a guide to center the racing cars across the 16½" (26.7cm) width of the 10½" × 16½" (26.7cm × 41.9cm) background blocks, placing them approximately ½" (1.3cm) up from the bottom raw edge. When you are happy with the orientation of the appliqué pieces, fuse them to the background blocks following the manufacturer's instructions.

   Repeat to center and fuse the stars to 16 assorted 5½" (14cm) background blocks.

4. Stitch around the appliqué pieces using your favorite method. (I used machine blanket stitch and matching thread.) Set aside.

Make the Four-Patch Blocks

1. Start with four 3" (7.6cm) squares, 2 solid white squares and 2 contrasting color squares. Lay out the squares to form a Four-Patch block. Use a ¼" (6mm) seam to sew the squares together in pairs; then sew the pairs together to make the finished block (Figure 2). Press well.

   Repeat to make 12 Four-Patch blocks: 3 red & white, 2 blue & white, 3 green & white and 4 orange & white.

Make the Quilt Center

1. Use Figure 3 as a guide to lay out the finished blocks. When you are happy with the placement and orientation of the blocks, first sew the Four-Patch blocks, star squares and 5½" (14cm) squares together in pairs (Figure 4). Then sew the joined blocks to the car blocks to make 5 horizontal rows. Press the seams in each row in opposite directions.

2. Once each row is sewn, pin and then sew the 5 rows together, carefully matching the seams, to make the center of the quilt. Press well, then set aside.

Figure 1

Figure 2

Figure 3

Figure 4

Figure 4   Figure 5

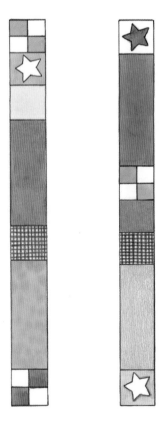

Figure 6   Figure 7

Make the Borders

1. To make the left border, sew 1 solid 5½"
   (14cm) square, 1 star block, one 5½" × 20½"
   (14cm × 52.1cm) red rectangle, 1 Four-Patch block,
   1 solid 5½" (14cm) square, and one 5½" × 10½"
   (14cm × 26.7cm) light blue rectangle together
   at the short ends. The strip will measure 50½"
   (128.3cm) long (Figure 4). Sew the border to the
   left-hand side of the quilt. Press the seam outward.

2. To make the right border, sew one 5½" × 15½"
   (14cm × 39.4cm) orange rectangle, 1 star block,
   one 5½" × 10½" (14cm × 26.7cm) red rectangle, 1 Four-Patch block and one 5½" × 15½"
   (14cm × 39.4cm) cornflower blue rectangle
   together at the short ends. The strip will measure
   50½" (128.3cm) long (Figure 5). Sew the border
   to the right-hand side of the quilt. Press the seam
   outward.

3. To make the top border, sew 1 Four-Patch block,
   1 star block, 1 solid 5½" (14cm) square, one
   5½" × 16½" (14cm × 41.9cm) red rectangle,
   1 solid 5½" (14cm) square, one 5½" × 16½"
   (14cm × 41.9cm) light blue rectangle and 1 Four-
   Patch block together at the short ends. The strip
   will measure 57½" (146.1cm) long (Figure 6). Sew
   the border to the top of the quilt. Press the seam
   outward.

4. To make the bottom border, sew 1 star block, one
   5½" × 16½" (14cm × 41.9cm) red rectangle, 1
   Four-Patch block, 2 solid 5½" (14cm) squares, one
   5½" × 16½" (14cm × 41.9cm) orange rectangle
   and 1 star block together at the short ends. The
   strip will measure 57½" (146.1cm) long (Figure 7).
   Sew the border to the bottom of the quilt. Press the
   seam outward.

Prepare the Backing

1. Sew the two 66½" (168.9cm) lengths of backing fabric together along the long edges, then
   trim to make a piece measuring approximately
   63½" × 66½" (161.3cm × 168.9cm).

Finish the Quilt

1. Layer the backing, batting and quilt top (see Making a Quilt Sandwich on page 15). Baste the layers together using your favorite method. Start quilting from the center and work your way out to the edges.

2. Sew the six 2½" (6.4cm) black & white medium checked strips together using straight seams.

Press them open. Fold the binding strip in half lengthwise, wrong sides facing, and press well.

Sew the binding to the front of the quilt using a ¼" (6mm) seam, and then sew the ends together where they meet. Wrap the binding to the back of the quilt and hand-stitch in place. Label and date your quilt to finish.

SPEEDY RACER
SOFT TOY

Finished Size: 19" (48.3cm) tall

Materials

¼ yard (23cm) of solid red fabric for the head, body, legs and appliqué

1 fat eighth (45.7cm × 27.9cm) of white-on-white fabric for the body, helmet, sleeves and appliqué

1 fat eighth (45.7cm × 27.9cm) of deep blue-on-blue fabric for the arms and back body

3½" × 7½" (8.9cm × 19.1cm) rectangle of medium blue-on-blue fabric for the helmet and appliqué

7½" × 12" (19.1cm × 30.5cm) rectangle of skin-colored fabric for the face and hands

8" (20.3m) square of black-on-black fabric for the body and shoes

3½" × 5½" (8.9cm × 14cm) rectangle of light blue-on-blue fabric for the visor

Scrap of solid yellow and solid brown fabric for the appliqué

Assorted Supplies

Light lead pencil

Fabric marking pen

Dark brown embroidery floss for the facial features

Matching thread to suit your favorite method of appliqué

12" (30.5cm) square of lightweight fusible web

2 small black buttons for eyes

Polyester fiberfill

Tracing paper (optional)

4 *Speedy Racer Soft Toy* template pages

Cutting

Trace and cut out the template pieces. You will need to trace the head, front body, back body, arm, hand, leg and shoe pieces. Pin the template pieces to the fabrics you have chosen and cut the following:

White-on-White Fabric

Cut (2) 3½" × 4½" (8.9cm × 11.4cm) rectangles for the body.

Cut (2) 1¼" × 7½" (3.2cm × 19.1cm) rectangles for the helmet.

Cut (1) 1½" × 15" (3.8cm × 38.1cm) rectangle for the arms.

Solid Red Fabric

Cut (1) 2½" × 7" (6.4cm × 17.8cm) rectangle for the body.

Cut (2) 3½" × 7½" (8.9cm × 19.1cm) rectangles for the helmet.

Cut 1 head piece.

Cut 4 leg pieces (cut 2 in reverse).

Black-on-Black Fabric

Cut (1) 1" × 4½" (2.5cm × 11.4cm) rectangle for the body.

Cut 4 shoe pieces (cut 2 in reverse).

Medium Blue-on-Blue Fabric

Cut (1) 1¼" × 7½" (3.2cm × 19.1cm) rectangle for the helmet.

Deep Blue-on-Blue Fabric

Cut (1) 5½" × 15" (14cm × 38.1cm) rectangle for the arms.

Cut 2 back body pieces (cut 1 in reverse).

Skin-Colored Fabric

Cut 4 hand pieces (cut 2 in reverse).

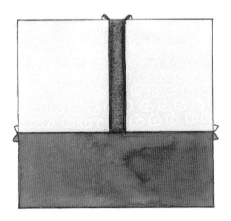

Figure 1

Make the Racer

Note: A short 1.5 stitch length and a ¼" (6mm) seam are used throughout.

1. Sew the 3½" × 4½" (8.9cm × 11.4cm) white-on-white rectangles to each side of the 1" × 4½" (2.5cm × 11.4cm) black-on-black rectangle, sewing along the long edges; press the seams toward the sides. Pin and then sew the 2½" × 7" (6.4cm × 17.8cm) solid red rectangle to the bottom edge. Press the seam open.

    Center and pin the front body template piece to the completed fabric unit, aligning the bottom edges of the template and the red fabric, and cut 1 front body piece (Figure 1). Set aside.

2. Sew the 1½" × 15" (3.8cm × 38.1cm) white-on-white rectangle to the 5½" × 15" (14cm × 38.1cm) deep blue-on-blue rectangle, sewing along the long edges. Press the seam open. Pin the arm template piece to the completed fabric unit, aligning the bottom edges of the template with the white fabric. Cut 4 arm pieces (2 in reverse) (Figure 2). Set them aside.

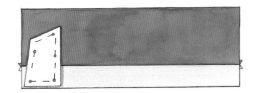

Figure 2

3. Sew the two 1¼" × 7½" (3.2cm × 19.1cm) white-on-white rectangles to each side of the 1¼" × 7½" (3.2cm × 19.1cm) medium blue-on-blue rectangle, sewing along the long edges. Sew a 3½" × 7½" (8.9cm × 19.1cm) solid red rectangle to either side of the striped unit. Press the seams toward the red fabric. Center and pin the head template piece to the completed fabric unit and cut out 1 back head piece (Figure 3).

Figure 3

4. Trace the required appliqué pieces from the template pages onto the paper side of the fusible webbing using a sharp pencil; leave approximately ½" (1.3cm) between each piece. Cut the pieces out roughly, leaving ¼" (6mm) of paper around each piece.

   You will need to trace the face, the visor, the hair, the helmet trim, 1 small star, 1 small circle and the number *1*.

5. Fuse the pieces to the fabrics you have chosen, following the manufacturer's instructions. Cut the pieces out carefully on the lines when cool. Remove the backing paper from the appliqué pieces, then use the templates as a guide to fuse the pieces to the head and body pieces.

Figure 4

6. Stitch around the appliqué pieces using your favorite method. (I used machine blanket stitch and matching thread.) Draw the mouth on the toy and backstitch using 2 strands of dark brown embroidery floss. Sew the buttons to the face for eyes using strong thread, then knot securely (Figure 4).

7. Pin and then sew the front head piece to the front body piece with right sides facing (Figure 5). Press the seams open. Set aside.

WATCH YOUR EDGES

Do not place the appliqué pieces too close to the raw edges of the helmet and body—they may get caught in the seams.

Figure 5

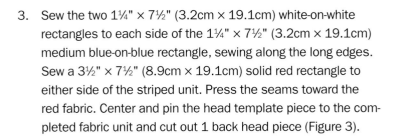

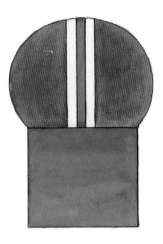

Figure 6

10. Sew the 2 back body pieces together with right sides facing. Leave the seam open where marked on the template. Press the seam open. Pin and then sew the back head piece to the joined back body pieces with right sides facing (Figure 6). Press the seam open. Set aside.

11. Sew the hands to the arms, then sew the arms together in pairs with right sides facing. Leave the top and side seams open where marked on the template. Notch the seam allowances on the curves and turn the arms right-side out through the top opening (Figure 7).

12. Sew the shoes and legs together in the same manner, then sew the legs together in pairs. Trim the corners, then turn the legs right-side out through the top opening (Figure 8).

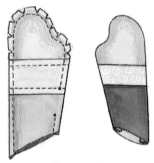

Figure 7

Figure 8

HiDiNg YOUR ALLOWANCE

Press the seams toward the darker fabric whenever possible throughout.

13. Place the front of the doll right-side up on your work surface. Use the template as a guide to position the arms and legs right sides down and facing inward on the body. Make sure the stuffing openings are facing downward on the arms and inward on the legs. Pin and then baste them to the doll. The arms and legs are not stuffed until the doll is completed (Figure 9).

14. Place the front of the doll right-side up on your work surface again. Fold the arms and legs in toward the center of the body. Place the back of the doll on top of the front of the doll with right sides facing. Pin the shapes together well to secure (Figure 10). Sew around the doll using a short stitch length and being careful to catch only the basted ends of the arms and legs in the seams.

15. Carefully notch the seam allowance on the curves, then gently turn the doll right-side out through the back opening. Stuff the body, arms and legs until firm. Hand-stitch the openings closed.

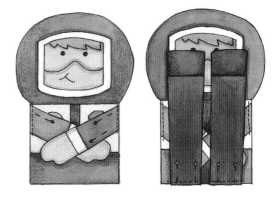

Figure 9

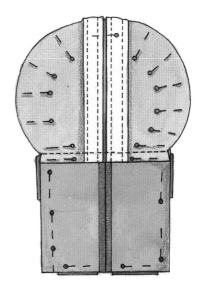

Figure 10

WiLD ThiNgs

QUiLT

There's no need to be afraid of monsters under the bed anymore, not when you have wild things tucking you in at night! Stitch up a few of the Wild Things Soft Toys and you'll never have to worry about things that go bump in the night again!

Finished Size: 54½" × 54½" (138.4cm × 138.4cm)

Materials

Background Blocks and Borders

⅜ yard (34cm) of black & white large dot fabric

⅜ yard (34cm) of gray & white small dot fabric

½ yard (0.5m) of solid gray fabric

1 yard (0.9m) of white-on-white fabric (also for the appliqué)

⅞ yard (0.8m) of black-on-black fabric for the background blocks and border

¼ yard (23cm) of white & black large dot fabric for the border

3" (7.6cm) × WOF each of red-on-red, green-on-green, solid purple and solid turquoise fabric for the inner border

Appliqué

½ yard (0.5m) total of assorted blue solid and print fabrics

¼ yard (23cm) total each of assorted yellow and pink solid and print fabrics

⅜ yard (34cm) total each of assorted purple, green, orange and red solid and print fabrics

Binding and Backing

6" (15.2cm) × WOF each of yellow-on-yellow, blue-on-blue, green-on-green and orange-on-orange prints for the binding

3⅜ yards (3.1m) of fabric for the backing

Assorted Supplies

Light lead pencil

Fabric marking pen

Matching thread to suit your favorite method of appliqué

60½" (153.7cm) square of batting

Approximately 5 yards (4.6cm) of lightweight fusible web (I used Heat n Bond Lite, which measures 17" [43cm] wide)

32 assorted large black buttons for the eyes

33 *Wild Things Quilt* template pages

Cutting

Black & White Large Dot Fabric

Cut (1) 11½" (29.2cm) × WOF strip. Subcut (3) 11½" (29.2cm) squares for the background blocks and (1) 4½" × 11½" (11.4cm × 29.2cm) rectangle for the border.

Gray & White Small Dot Fabric

Cut (1) 11½" (29.2cm) × WOF strip. Subcut (2) 11½" (29.2cm) squares for the background blocks; (2) 4½" × 11½" (11.4cm × 29.2cm) rectangles and (1) 5½" (14cm) square for the border.

Solid Gray Fabric

Cut (1) 11½" (29.2cm) × WOF strip. Subcut (3) 11½" (29.2cm) squares for the background blocks and (1) 5½" (14cm) square for the border.

Cut (1) 4½" (11.4cm) × WOF strip. Subcut (2) 4½" × 11½" (11.4cm × 29.2cm) rectangles for the border.

White-on-White Fabric

Cut (2) 11½" (29.2cm) × WOF strips. Subcut (4) 11½" (29.2cm) squares for the background blocks.

Black-on-Black Fabric

Cut (2) 11½" (29.2cm) × WOF strips. Subcut (4) 11½" (29.2cm) squares for the background blocks.

Cut (6) 4½" × 11½" (11.4cm × 29.2cm) rectangles and (1) 5½" (14cm) square for the border.

White & Black Large Dot Fabric

Cut (1) 5½" (14cm) square for the border.

Cut (5) 4½" × 11½" (11.4cm × 29.2cm) rectangles for the borders.

Inner Border Fabrics (Red, Green, Purple and Blue)

Cut (2) 1½" (3.8cm) × WOF strips from each fabric.

Binding Fabric (Yellow, Blue, Green and Orange)

Cut (2) 3" (7.6cm) × WOF strips from each fabric.

Backing Fabric

Cut (2) 60½" (153.7cm) lengths. Remove the selvages.

Figure 1

Make the Appliqué Blocks

1. Trace the required appliqué pieces from the template pages onto the paper side of the fusible webbing using a sharp pencil; leave approximately ½" (1.3cm) between each piece.

   You will need to trace 16 large wild things and 1 small wild thing.

2. Cut the pieces out roughly, leaving ¼" (6mm) of paper around each piece. Fuse the pieces to the fabrics you have chosen for the appliqué following the manufacturer's instructions. Cut the pieces out carefully on the lines when cool.

3. Remove the backing paper from the appliqué pieces and use Figure 1 and the templates as a guide to place the wild things on the background blocks. The

bottom raw edges of the wild things' bodies align with the bottom raw edges of the background blocks. When you are happy with the position of the appliqué pieces, fuse them to the background blocks following the manufacturer's instructions.

4. Stitch around the appliqué pieces using your favorite method. (I used machine blanket stitch and matching thread.)

Make the Quilt Center

1. Lay out the finished wild thing blocks into 4 rows, each with 4 blocks. When you are happy with the placement of the blocks, sew each horizontal row of 4 blocks together and press the seams in each row in opposite directions. Once each row is sewn, pin and then sew the 4 rows together, carefully matching the seams, to make the center of the quilt. Press well, then set aside (Figure 2).

Make the Borders

1. Sew the 1½" (3.8cm) red-on-red, green-on-green, solid purple and solid turquoise fabric strips together in matching pairs, using diagonal seams. Trim the seams to ¼" (6mm) and press them open. Trim each strip to measure 44½" (113cm). Set all aside.

2. To make the borders, sew four 4½" × 11½" (11.4cm × 29.2cm) rectangles together end to end. Make 4 border strips, each measuring 44½" (113cm) long. Press the seams in 1 direction. Pin and then sew the 1½" × 44½" (3.8cm × 113cm) red, green, purple and turquoise fabric strips to the pieced border strips with right sides facing (Figure 3). Press the seams toward the narrow borders.

3. Sew the turquoise border to the left side of the quilt and the green border to the right side of the quilt. Make sure the colored strips are abutting the quilt center. Press the seams outward.

4. Sew the 5½" (14cm) squares to each end of the remaining 2 border strips (Figure 4). Press the seams inward toward the border. You now have 2 strips that measure 54½" (138.4cm) long.

Figure 2

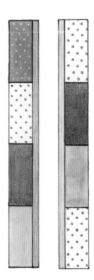

Figure 3

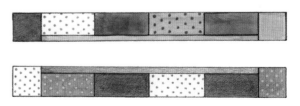

Figure 4

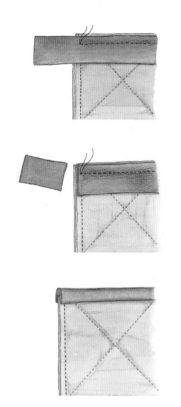

Figure 5

5. Sew the red border to the top of the quilt and the purple border to the bottom of the quilt, carefully matching the seams. Press the seams outward.

Prepare the Backing

1. Sew the two 60½" (153.7cm) lengths of backing fabric together along the long edges, then trim to make a piece measuring approximately 60½" (153.7cm) square.

Finish the Quilt

1. Layer the backing, batting and quilt top (see Making a Quilt Sandwich on page 15). Baste the layers together using your favorite method. Start quilting from the center and work your way out to the edges.

2. Sew the two 3" (7.6cm) yellow-on-yellow, blue-on-blue, green-on-green and orange-on-orange binding strips together in matching pairs using diagonal seams. Trim the seams to ¼" (6mm) and press them open. Fold each binding strip in half lengthwise, wrong sides facing, and press well. This will give you 4 binding strips.

3. Sew the yellow binding strip to the left-hand edge of the quilt top using a ½" (1.3cm) seam. Trim the ends of the binding even with the edges of the quilt. Wrap the binding to the back of the quilt and hand-stitch it in place (Figure 5). Repeat to sew the orange binding strip to the right-hand edge of the quilt.

4. Sew the green binding strip to the top of the quilt, making sure the binding extends ¾" (1.9cm) past the edges on both sides. Tuck the overhanging tails of binding to the back of the quilt and baste in place. Wrap the remainder of the binding to the back of the quilt and hand-stitch it in place (Figure 6). Repeat to sew the blue binding strip to the bottom of the quilt.

5. Use the photo at the end of the project and the templates as a guide to sew the buttons to the wild things for eyes. Sew the buttons in place through all thicknesses of the quilt using strong thread. Knot securely. Label and date your quilt to finish.

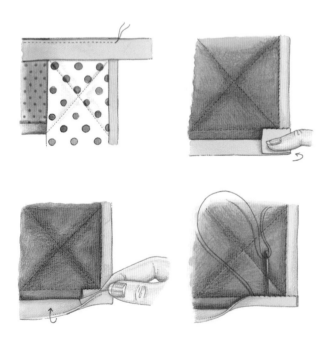

Figure 6

WILD THING
SOFT TOY

Finished Size: 15" (38.1cm) tall

Materials

Violet & Pink Wild Thing

1 fat quarter (45.7cm × 55.9cm) of bright pink corduroy for the body and arms

1 fat eighth (45.7cm × 27.9cm) of bright purple corduroy for the head and legs

6" (15.2cm) square of white wool felt for the eyes and teeth

8" (20.3cm) square of orange & white dot fabric for the horns

2 small black buttons for the eyes

Blue Wild Thing

10" × 16" (25.4cm × 40.6cm) rectangle of blue-on-blue fabric for the body

6" × 8" (15.2cm × 20.3cm) rectangle of blue-green fabric for the head

12" (30.5cm) square of solid yellow fabric for the arms

10" × 16" (25.4cm × 40.6cm) rectangle of yellow & blue dot fabric for the legs

8" (20.3cm) square of red & orange dot fabric for the horns

5" (12.7cm) square of white wool felt for the eye and teeth

Scrap of green-on-green fabric for the eye

Scrap of black wool felt for the eye

Assorted Supplies (for both dolls)

Light lead pencil

Fabric marking pen

Matching thread to suit your favorite method of appliqué

8" (20.3cm) square of lightweight fusible web

Polyester fiberfill

Tracing paper (optional)

6 *Wild Thing Soft Toy* template pages

113

Cutting for the Violet & Pink Wild Thing

Trace and cut out the template pieces. You will need to trace the head, front body, back body, arm, leg and horn pieces. Pin the template pieces to the fabrics you have chosen and cut the following:

Bright Pink Corduroy

Cut 1 front body piece.

Cut 2 back body pieces (cut 1 in reverse).

Cut 4 arm pieces (cut 2 in reverse).

Bright Purple Corduroy

Cut 1 head piece.

Cut 4 leg pieces (cut 2 in reverse).

Orange & White Dot Fabric

Cut 4 horn pieces (cut 2 in reverse).

Cutting for the Blue Wild Thing

Blue-on-Blue Fabric

Cut 1 front body piece.

Cut 2 back body pieces (cut 1 in reverse).

Blue-Green Fabric

Cut 1 head piece.

Yellow Fabric

Cut 4 arm pieces (cut 2 in reverse).

Yellow & Blue Dot Fabric

Cut 4 leg pieces (cut 2 in reverse).

Red & Orange Dot Fabric

Cut 4 horn pieces (cut 2 in reverse).

Figure 1

Figure 2

Make the Wild Thing

Note: A short 1.5 stitch length and a ¼" (6mm) seam are used throughout.

1. Trace the appropriate eye and teeth pieces from the template pages onto the paper side of the fusible webbing using a sharp pencil; leave ½" (1.3cm) between each piece. Cut the pieces out roughly, leaving ¼" (6mm) of paper around each piece.

2. Fuse the pieces to the felt or fabric you have chosen following the manufacturer's instructions. Cut the pieces out carefully on the lines when cool. Remove the backing paper from the appliqué pieces and use the templates as a guide to fuse them to the front head or body piece. The teeth are appliquéd to the head piece when making the violet & pink wild thing. The teeth are appliquéd to the front body piece when making the blue wild thing.

    Stitch around the appliqué pieces using your favorite method. (I used machine blanket stitch and matching thread.) Sew the buttons to the face for eyes, where appropriate, using strong thread, then knot securely (Figure 1).

3. Pin and then sew the head piece to the front body piece. Press well (Figure 2).

4. Sew the horn pieces together in pairs with right sides facing. Leave the bottom edge open where marked on the template. Notch the seam allowances on the curves and turn the horns right-side out. Stuff the horns semi-firmly, leaving approximately ½" (1.3cm) at the opening unstuffed.

5. Use the template as a guide to position the horns right sides down and facing inward on the head piece. Pin then baste them to the front of the wild thing (Figure 3).

Figure 3

6. Sew the 2 back body pieces together with right sides facing. Leave the seam open where marked on the template. Press the seam open.

7. Sew the arms together in pairs with right sides facing. Leave the top and side seams open where marked on the template. Notch the seam allowances on the curves and turn the arms right-side out through the top opening.

   Sew the legs together, notch the seams and turn the legs right side out in the same manner.

8. Place the front of the wild thing right-side up on your work surface. Use the template as a guide to position the arms and legs facing inward on the body. Make sure the stuffing openings are facing downward on the arms and inward on the legs. Pin and then baste them to the body. The arms and legs are not stuffed until the toy is completed (Figure 4).

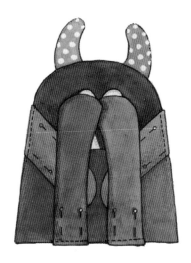

Figure 4

9. Place the front of the toy right-side up on your work surface again. Fold the horns, arms and legs in toward the center of the body. Place the back of the wild thing on top of the front of the wild thing with right sides facing. Pin the shapes together to secure. Sew around the toy using a short stitch length, being careful to catch only the basted ends of the horns, arms and legs in the seams. Backstitch at the beginning and end of the seam.

10. Fold 1 bottom corner of the body so the side and bottom seams are centered on top of each other; pin. Stitch across the triangle formed by this fold, sewing approximately ¾" (1.9cm) in from the pointy edge. Sew across the seam twice to strengthen the base. Repeat to sew the opposite bottom corner. Trim the corners approximately ¼" (6mm) from the stitching line (Figure 5).

Figure 5

11. Carefully notch the seam allowances on the curves then gently turn the toy right-side out through the back opening. Stuff the body, arms and legs until firm. Hand-stitch the openings closed.

PURRRFECTLY PRETTY KITTIES
QUILT

This adorable quilt features purrrfectly pretty kitties playing in a garden of flowers and Nine Patch blocks. Use the templates from the Snuggle Bears Quilt to add some bees and butterflies to the garden, but watch out for Miss Kitty—she's getting ready to pounce!

Finished Size: 63" × 75½" (160cm × 191.8cm)

Materials

Background and Nine Patch Blocks

⅜ yard (34cm) each of blue & white large dot fabric, blue & white medium checked fabric, medium orange fabric, yellow & white small checked fabric and medium yellow print fabric

6" (15.2cm) × WOF strip each of blue & white small dot fabric, orange & white small print fabric and solid yellow fabric

3" (7.6cm) × WOF strip of blue & white small checked fabric

½ yard (0.5m) of green & white floral print fabric

⅝ yard (0.6m) each of green & white medium checked fabric and medium pink-on-pink fabric

1 yard (0.9m) of solid white fabric

Appliqué

⅜ yard (34cm) each of black-on-black print fabric, solid gray fabric and brown-on-brown fabric

½ yard (0.5m) each of white-on-white fabric and orange-on-orange fabric

¼ yard (23cm) of cream-on-cream fabric

1 fat eighth (45.7cm × 27.9cm) each of green-on-green fabric and medium pink-on-pink fabric

10" (25.4cm) square of yellow & white dot fabric

6" (15.2cm) square of turquoise & white dot fabric

Scraps of turquoise, light blue, pink, orange, green, purple, red and dark gray fabrics

Binding and Backing

⅝ yard (0.6m) of blue-on-blue fabric for the binding

4⅝ yards (4.2m) of fabric for the backing

Assorted Supplies

Light lead pencil

Fabric marking pen

Black, brown and white embroidery floss for the facial features

Matching thread to suit your favorite method of appliqué

69" × 81½" (175.3cm × 207cm) piece of batting

Approximately 6½ yards (5.9m) of lightweight fusible web (I used Heat n Bond Lite, which measures 17" [43cm] wide)

16 pairs of assorted small buttons for the cats' eyes

5 pairs of assorted tiny buttons for the kittens' and mice's eyes

19 jewel buttons for the cats' collars

9 *Purrrfectly Pretty Kitties Quilt* template pages

Cutting

Blue & White Large Dot Fabric

Cut (1) 13" (33cm) × WOF strip. Subcut (3) 13" (33cm) squares for the background blocks.

Blue & White Medium Checked Fabric

Cut (1) 13" (33cm) × WOF strip. Subcut (2) 13" (33cm) squares for the background blocks.

From the remaining fabric, cut (14) 2⅝" (6.7cm) squares for the Nine Patch blocks.

Blue & White Small Dot Fabric

Cut (2) 2⅝" (6.7cm) × WOF strips. Subcut (20) 2⅝" (6.7cm) squares for the Nine Patch blocks.

Blue & White Small Checked Fabric

Cut (1) 2⅝" (6.7cm) × WOF strip. Subcut (9) 2⅝" (6.7cm) squares for the Nine Patch blocks.

Green & White Floral Print Fabric

Cut (1) 2⅝" (6.7cm) × WOF strip. Subcut (14) 2⅝" (6.7cm) squares for the Nine Patch blocks.

Cut (1) 13" (33cm) × WOF strip. Subcut (2) 13" (33cm) squares for the background blocks. From the remaining fabric, cut (10) 2⅝" (6.7cm) squares for the Nine Patch blocks.

Green & White Medium Checked Fabric

Cut (1) 13" (33cm) × WOF strip. Subcut (3) 13" (33cm) squares for the background blocks.

Cut (2) 2⅝" (6.7cm) × WOF strips. Subcut (25) 2⅝" (6.7cm) squares for the Nine Patch blocks.

Medium Pink-on-Pink Fabric

Cut (1) 13" (33cm) × WOF strip. Subcut (3) 13" (33cm) squares for the background blocks.

Cut (2) 2⅝" (6.7cm) × WOF strips. Subcut (24) 2⅝" (6.7cm) squares for the Nine Patch blocks.

Medium Orange Fabric

Cut (1) 13" (33cm) × WOF strip. Subcut (2) 13" (33cm) squares for the background blocks.

Orange & White Small Print Fabric

Cut (2) 2⅝" (6.7cm) × WOF strips. Subcut (22) 2⅝" (6.7cm) squares for the Nine Patch blocks.

Yellow & White Small Checked Fabric

Cut (1) 13" (33cm) × WOF strip. Subcut (2) 13" (33cm) squares for the background blocks.
From the remaining fabric, cut (14) 2⅝" (6.7cm) squares for the Nine Patch blocks.

Medium Yellow Print Fabric

Cut (1) 13" (33cm) × WOF strip. Subcut (3) 13" (33cm) squares for the background blocks.

Solid Yellow Fabric

Cut (2) 2⅝" (6.7cm) × WOF strips. Subcut (28) 2⅝" (6.7cm) squares for the Nine Patch blocks.

Solid White Fabric

Cut (13) 2⅝" (6.7cm) × WOF strips. Subcut (180) 2⅝" (6.7cm) squares for the Nine Patch blocks.

Binding Fabric

Cut (8) 2½" (6.4cm) × WOF strips.

Backing Fabric

Cut (2) 81½" (207cm) lengths. Remove the selvages.

Make the Appliqué Blocks

1. Trace the required appliqué pieces from the template pages onto the paper side of the fusible webbing using a sharp pencil; leave approximately ½" (1.3cm) between each piece.

   You will need to trace 16 cats, 3 kittens, 2 mice and 15 flowers plus their centers and stems. Five flowers have long stems and 10 flowers have short stems.

2. Cut the pieces out roughly, leaving ¼" (6mm) of paper around each piece. Fuse the pieces to the fabrics you have chosen for the appliqué following the manufacturer's instructions. Cut the pieces out carefully on the lines when cool. You will need 4 black cats, 4 ginger cats, 4 cream cats and 4 gray cats.

3. Remove the backing paper from the appliqué pieces and use Figure 1 and the templates as a guide to place the cats and flowers on the background blocks. The bottom raw edges of the bodies, paws and flower stems align with the bottom raw edges of the background blocks. When you are happy with the position of the appliqué pieces, fuse them to the background blocks following the manufacturer's instructions. The flowers have been placed at different heights to add visual interest.

4. Stitch around the appliqué pieces using your favorite method. (I used machine blanket stitch and matching thread.) Use the templates as a guide to draw the features on each animal using a fine-point fabric pen. Backstitch the features using 2 strands of contrasting embroidery floss.

Make the Quilt Center

1. Lay out the finished cat and flower blocks into 5 rows, each with 4 blocks (Figure 2). When you are happy with the placement of the blocks, sew each horizontal row of blocks together and press the seams in each row in opposite directions.

2. Once each row is sewn, pin and then sew the 5 rows together, carefully matching the seams, to make the center of the quilt. Press well, then set aside.

Figure 1

Figure 2

Make the Nine Patch Borders

1. Use the photo at the end of the project as a guide to sort the 2⅝" (6.7cm) squares into 40 groups of 9 squares. Twenty groups are made up of 4 white squares and 5 matching colored squares, and 20 groups are made up of 5 white squares and 4 matching colored squares.

2. Choose a group of 9 squares and lay them out on your work surface in the shape of the Nine Patch block. Sew the squares together into 3 horizontal rows. Press the seams toward the darker fabric (Figure 3).

3. Sew the 3 rows together to make the block. Press the seams in the direction that will allow the border seams to butt together. Trim the block evenly on all sides to measure 6¾" (17.1cm) (Figure 4).

4. Repeat to make 40 Nine Patch blocks (20 with 4 white squares and 20 with 5 white squares).

5. To make the borders, sew 10 Nine Patch blocks together end to end, carefully matching the seams. Make 4 borders, each measuring 63" (160cm) long.

6. Sew a border strip to the left and right sides of the quilt. Press the seams outward. Sew the remaining 2 borders to the top and bottom of the quilt. Press the seams outward.

Prepare the Backing

1. Sew the two 81½" (207cm) lengths of backing fabric together along the long edges, then trim to make a piece measuring approximately 69" × 81½" (175.3cm × 207cm).

Finish the Quilt

1. Layer the backing, batting and quilt top (see Making a Quilt Sandwich on page 15). Baste the layers together using your favorite method. Start quilting from the center and work your way out to the edges.

2. Sew the eight 2½" (6.4cm) binding strips together using diagonal seams. Trim the seams to ¼" (6mm) and press them open. Fold the binding strip in half lengthwise, wrong sides facing, and press well.

   Sew the binding to the front of the quilt using a ¼" (6mm) seam, and then sew the ends together where they meet. Wrap the binding to the back of the quilt and hand-stitch in place.

3. Sew buttons to the animals' faces for eyes, and sew a button to each collar where indicated on the templates. Sew the buttons in place through all thicknesses of the quilt using strong thread. Knot securely. Label and date your quilt to finish.

Figure 3

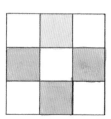

Figure 4

MiSS KiTTY
SOfT TOY

Finished Size: 22" (55.9cm) tall

Materials

⅜ yard (34cm) of linen-colored fabric for the head, paws, legs and ears

1 fat eighth (45.7cm × 27.9cm) of light pink-on-pink tiny dot fabric for the body, arms and ears

1½" × 15" (3.8cm × 38.1cm) strip of light blue & white striped fabric for the body

4" × 15" (10.2cm × 38.1cm) rectangle of medium pink-on-pink large dot fabric for the body

5" × 24½" (12.7cm × 62.2cm) rectangle of aqua & white dot fabric for the scarf

Scrap of red-on-red fabric for the heart

Assorted Supplies

Light lead pencil

Fabric marking pen

Light pink, charcoal gray and silver-gray embroidery floss for the facial features

Matching thread to suit your favorite method of appliqué

Scrap of lightweight fusible web

2½" × 24½" (6.4cm × 62.2cm) rectangle of batting for the scarf

13" (33cm) piece of medium-thick cotton cord or a white shoelace for the tail

2 small brown buttons for the eyes

1 decorative button for the scarf

Polyester fiberfill

Tracing paper (optional)

4 *Miss Kitty Soft Toy* template pages

Cutting

Trace and cut out the template pieces. You will need to trace the head, front body, back body, arm, paw and leg pieces. Pin the template pieces to the fabrics you have chosen and cut the following:

Linen-Colored Fabric

Cut 2 ear pieces (cut 1 in reverse).

Cut 2 head pieces (cut 1 in reverse).

Cut 4 paw pieces (cut 2 in reverse).

Cut 4 leg pieces (cut 2 in reverse).

Light Pink-on-Pink Dot Fabric

Cut (1) 2¾" × 15" (6.7cm × 38.1cm) rectangle for the body.

Cut 2 ear pieces (cut 2 in reverse).

Cut 4 arm pieces (cut 2 in reverse).

Light Blue & White Striped Fabric

Cut (1) 1½" × 15" (3.8cm × 38.1cm) rectangle for the body.

Medium Pink-on-Pink Dot Fabric

Cut (1) 4" × 15" (10.2cm × 38.1cm) rectangle for the body.

Aqua & White Dot Fabric

Cut (2) 2½" × 24¼" (6.4cm × 62.2cm) rectangles for the scarf.

Batting

Cut (1) 2½" × 24¼" (6.4cm × 62.2cm) rectangle for the scarf.

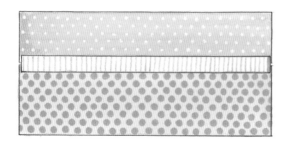

Figure 1

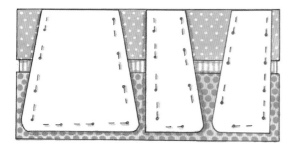

Figure 2

Make the Kitty

Note: A short 1.5 stitch length and a ¼" (6mm) seam are used throughout.

1. Sew the light pink-on-pink dot rectangle, the light blue & white striped rectangle and the medium pink-on-pink dot rectangle together along the long edges (Figure 1). Press well the seams toward the striped fabric.

2. Pin the front and back body template pieces to the completed fabric unit, aligning the top edges of the template and the light pink-on-pink fabric. Cut 1 front body piece and 2 back body pieces, remembering to cut 1 back body piece in reverse (Figure 2).

5. Trace the nose and heart pieces from the template page onto the paper side of the fusible webbing using a sharp pencil; leave approximately ½" (1.3cm) between each piece. Cut the pieces out roughly, leaving ¼" (6mm) of paper around the piece.

6. Fuse the nose and heart to your chosen fabrics following the manufacturer's instructions and cut them out carefully on the lines when cool. Remove the backing paper from the nose and use the template as a guide to fuse it to the front head piece. Set the heart aside.

7. Stitch around the nose using your favorite appliqué method. (I used machine blanket stitch and matching thread.) Draw the mouth and whiskers on the cat; then backstitch the mouth using 2 strands of charcoal embroidery floss and backstitch the whiskers using 2 strands of silver-gray embroidery floss. Sew the buttons to the face for eyes using strong thread, then knot securely.

8. Sew the ears together in pairs, a linen-colored ear to a pink-on-pink dot ear, with right sides facing. Leave the bottom edge open where marked on the template. Notch the seam allowances on the curves and turn the ears right-side out through the opening. Press gently. Make a small pleat in the center of each ear and baste the pleats in place (Figure 3).

9. Use the template as a guide to position the ears, pink sides down and facing inward, on the front head piece. Pin and then baste them in place (Figure 4).

10. Pin and then sew the front head piece to the front body piece with right sides facing (Figure 5). Press the seams open. Set it aside.

Figure 3

Figure 4

Figure 5

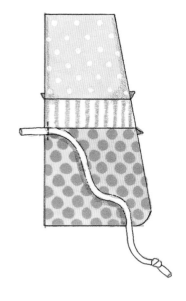

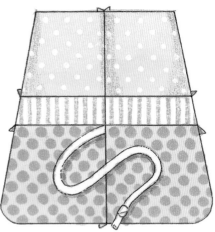

Figure 6

11. Tie a knot in the end of the tail. Use the template as a guide to position the tail on 1 of the back body pieces. Leave approximately 1" (2.5cm) overhang on the tail. Pin and then baste the tail to the back body piece (Figure 6).

12. Sew the 2 back body pieces together with right sides facing. Leave the seam open where marked on the template. Press the seam open (Figure 6). Pin and then sew the back head piece to the joined back body pieces with right sides facing (Figure 7). Press the seams open.

13. Sew the paws to the arms, then sew the arms together in pairs with right sides facing. Leave the top and side seams open where marked on the template. Notch the seam allowances on the curves and turn the arms right-side out through the top opening.

14. Sew the legs together in the same manner, leaving the top and side seams open where marked. Notch the seam allowances on the curves and turn the legs right-side out through the opening.

STRENGTHEN SEAMS

Backstitch at the beginning and end of each seam to strengthen the stitching.

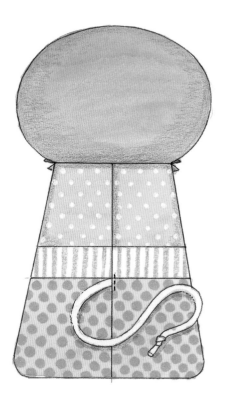

Figure 7

15. Place the front of the cat right-side up on your work surface. Use the template as a guide to position the arms and legs right sides down and facing inward on the body. Make sure the stuffing openings are facing downward on the arms and inward on the legs. Pin and then baste them to the cat. The arms and legs are not stuffed until the cat is completed (Figure 8).

16. Place the front of the cat right side-up on your work surface again. Fold the ears, arms and legs in toward the center of the body. Place the back of the cat on top of the front of the cat with right sides facing. Pin the shapes together to secure. Sew around the cat using a short stitch length, being careful to catch only the basted ends of the ears, arms and legs in the seams (Figure 9).

17. Carefully notch the seam allowance on the curves, then gently turn the toy right-side out through the back opening. Stuff the body, arms and legs until firm. Hand-stitch the openings closed.

18. Fuse the heart to the end of 1 aqua & white dot scarf piece, making sure to allow for the seams on the edges. Stitch around the heart as before.

19. Place the two 2½" × 24½" (6.4cm × 62.2cm) aqua & white dot rectangles together with right sides facing. Place the strip of batting on top and pin the pieces together. Stitch around the 4 sides, leaving a small opening on 1 long edge for turning. Clip the corners and turn the scarf right-side out. Hand-stitch the opening closed. Press gently.

    Stitch a decorative button to the center of the heart appliqué, then tie the scarf around the kitty's neck to finish.

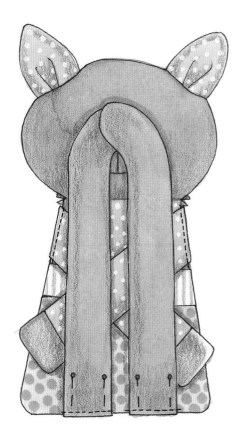

Figure 8

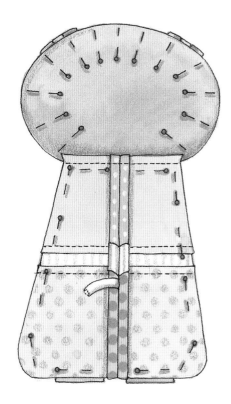

Figure 9

LITTLE ROBOTS
QUILT

Fall cogs over wheels for these adorable robots. Sew up a Little Robot Soft Toy to keep you company. The only thing it can't do is clean up your room!

Finished Size: 55½" × 67½" (141cm × 171.5cm)

Materials

Background Blocks
3 yards (2.7m) of red-on-red star fabric (also for the border)

Sashing
⅛ yard (11cm) each of 2 bright blue print fabrics, 2 bright yellow print fabrics and 4 black & white print fabrics

Appliqué and Borders
⅛ yard (11cm) of red & white dot fabric

¼ yard (23cm) total each of assorted black & white print and purple print fabrics

½ yard (0.5m) of solid white fabric

⅜ yard (34cm) total of assorted orange print fabrics

⅝ yard (0.6m) total each of assorted yellow, blue and green print fabrics

Binding and Backing
½ yard (0.5m) of bright blue-on-blue fabric for the binding

4⅛ yards (3.8m) of fabric for the backing

Assorted Supplies
Light lead pencil

Chalk pencil

Fabric marking pen

Black and brown embroidery floss for the facial features

Matching thread to suit your favorite method of appliqué 61½" × 73½" (156.2cm × 186.7cm) piece of batting

Approximately 8 yards (7.3m) of lightweight fusible web (I used Heat n Bond Lite, which measures 17" [43cm] wide)

12 pairs of assorted small black buttons for the robots' eyes

29 assorted small colored buttons for the robots' bodies

6 tiny brown buttons for the robot cat's whiskers

18 *Little Robots Quilt* template pages

Cutting

Red-on-Red Star Fabric

Cut (4) 14½" (36.8cm) × WOF strips. Subcut (12) 11½" × 14½" (29.2cm × 36.8cm) rectangles for the background blocks.

Cut (6) 1½" (3.8cm) × WOF strips.

Cut (6) 2" (5.1cm) × WOF strips.

Cut (4) 2½" (6.4cm) × WOF strips. Subcut (56) 2½" (6.4cm) squares.

Cut (8) 5½" × 11½" (14cm × 29.2cm) rectangles from the remaining fabric.

Assorted Yellow, Orange, Blue, Green and Purple Fabric

Cut a total of (56) 2½" (6.4cm) squares.

Sashing Fabric

From each of the 2 blue fabrics, 2 yellow fabrics and 4 black & white fabrics, cut (2) 1½" (3.8cm) × WOF strips.

Binding Fabric

Cut (7) 2½" (6.4cm) × WOF strips.

Backing Fabric

Cut (2) 73½" (186.7cm) lengths. Remove the selvages.

Make the Appliqué Blocks

1. Trace the required appliqué pieces from the template pages onto the paper side of the fusible webbing using a sharp pencil; leave approximately ½" (1.3cm) between each piece.

   You will need to trace 12 robots, 14 cogs and 8 wheels.

2. Cut the pieces out roughly, leaving ¼" (6mm) of paper around each piece. Fuse the pieces to the fabrics you have chosen for the appliqué following the manufacturer's instructions. Cut the pieces out carefully on the lines when cool. Set the cogs and wheels aside.

3. Measure ½" (1.3cm) in from each of the 4 raw edges of the background block, and lightly mark the lines using a chalk pencil. Remove the backing paper from the robot appliqué pieces and use Figure 1 and the templates as a guide to place the robots on the background blocks.

   When you are happy with placement of the robots, fuse each robot to a background block following the manufacturer's instructions. Align the bottom of the feet with the bottom chalk line, and place the head and arms within the top and side chalk lines

(Figure 1). (This prevents the appliqué from being caught in the seams.)

4. Stitch around the appliqué shapes using your favorite method. (I used hand-stitched blanket stitch and 2 strands of matching embroidery floss.)

5. Use the templates as a guide to draw the body and antenna markings on each of the robots using a fine-point fabric pen. Use 2 strands of black or brown embroidery floss to chainstitch the antenna and to backstitch the facial features, dials and words. Press the blocks and set aside.

Figure 1

Make the Cog and Wheel Rows

1. Sew four 5½" × 11½" (14cm × 29.2cm) red rectangles together end to end to make a long strip. Press the seams open to distribute the bulk. Repeat to make 2 background strips.

2. Use Figure 2 as a guide to fuse 7 cogs and 4 wheels evenly along the length of each background strip. Remember not to place the appliqué pieces too close to the ends of the strips—they will get caught in the seams. Stitch around the appliqué pieces as before.

Make the Quilt Center

1. Use the photo at the end of this project and Figure 3 as a guide to lay out the robot blocks into 3 rows, each with 4 blocks. When you are happy with the placement of the blocks, sew each horizontal row of 4 blocks together. Press the seams in 1 direction.

2. The finished robot and cog rows should measure approximately 44½" (113cm) in length. If the lengths of the rows vary by more than ¼" (6mm), you will need to adjust them to size. To adjust the robot rows, unpick some of the seams and resew using smaller or larger seams to fit. Adjust the cog and wheel rows (if necessary) by trimming them evenly at the short ends, being careful not to trim too close to the appliqué.

3. Sew the 1½" (3.8cm) blue, yellow and black & white print sashing strips together into matching pairs using diagonal seams. Trim the seams to ¼" (6mm) and press them open. Set 2 black & white strips aside. Cut two 44½" (113cm) strips each from the blue, yellow and remaining black & white sashing strips.

4. Use the photo at the end of this project and Figure 3 as a guide to lay out the rows of robots, cogs and sashing strips. Pin and then sew the rows together. Press the seams toward the sashing strips.

5. Measure the length of the quilt through the center and cut the remaining 2 black & white sashing strips to this measurement. Pin and then sew the sashing strips to the left- and right-hand edges of the quilt. Press the seams toward the sashing strips.

Figure 2

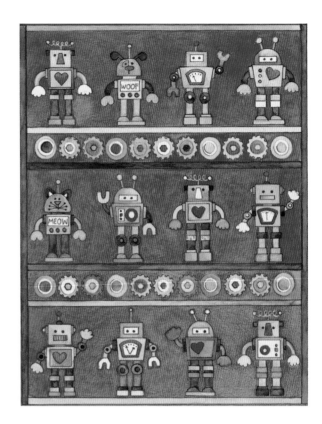

Figure 3

MEASURE FIRST

Before cutting the fabric for the sashing strips, check the measurements of your own quilt to be accurate.

Make the Border

1. Sew six 1½" (3.8cm) red strips together using diagonal seams. Trim the seams to ¼" (6mm) and press them open. Repeat to sew the six 2" (5.1cm) red strips together. Set them aside.

2. Measure the width of the quilt through the center and cut two 1½" (3.8cm) strips to this measurement. Pin and then sew them to the top and bottom of the quilt. Press the seams outward.

   Measure the length of the quilt through the center and cut 2 strips to this measurement. Pin and then sew them to each side of the quilt. Press the seams outward.

3. To make the top and bottom borders, sew 12 red and 12 randomly selected contrasting color 2½" (6.4cm) squares together. Start sewing with a red square and alternate the colors as you sew. Press the seams toward the red fabric. Make 2 strips measuring 48½" (123.2cm). Use the photograph on the following page as a guide to sew them to the top and bottom of the quilt. Press the seams outward.

4. To make the side borders, sew 16 red and 16 contrasting color 2½" (6.4cm) squares together. Make 2 strips measuring 64½" (163.8cm). Sew these to each side of the quilt, ensuring the checked pattern continues around the quilt in sequence. Press the seams outward.

5. Measure the width of the quilt through the center and cut two 2" (5.1cm) strips (set aside in Step 1 of Make the Border) to this measurement. Pin and then sew them to the top and bottom of the quilt. Press the seams outward.

   Measure the length of the quilt through the center and cut two 2" (5.1cm) strips to this measurement. Pin and then sew them to each side of the quilt. Press the seams outward.

Prepare the Backing

1. Sew the two 73½" (186.7cm) lengths of backing fabric together along the long edges. Trim to make a piece measuring approximately 61½" × 73½" (156.2cm × 186.7cm).

Finish the Quilt

1. Layer the backing, batting and quilt top (see Making a Quilt Sandwich on page 15). Baste the layers together using your favorite method. Start quilting from the center and work your way out to the edges.

2. Sew the seven 2½" (6.4cm) binding strips together using diagonal seams. Trim the seams to ¼" (6mm) and press them open. Fold the binding strip in half lengthwise, wrong sides facing, and press well. Sew the binding to the front of the quilt using a ¼" (6mm) seam, then sew the ends together where they meet. Wrap the binding to the back and hand-stitch in place.

3. Sew buttons to the robots' faces for eyes and to the bodies of the robots. Sew the buttons in place through all thicknesses of the quilt using strong thread. Knot securely. Label and date your quilt to finish.

HOW TO MEASURE

When measuring a quilt, always measure through the center to make sure the borders will be the correct size and to avoid creating wavy edges.

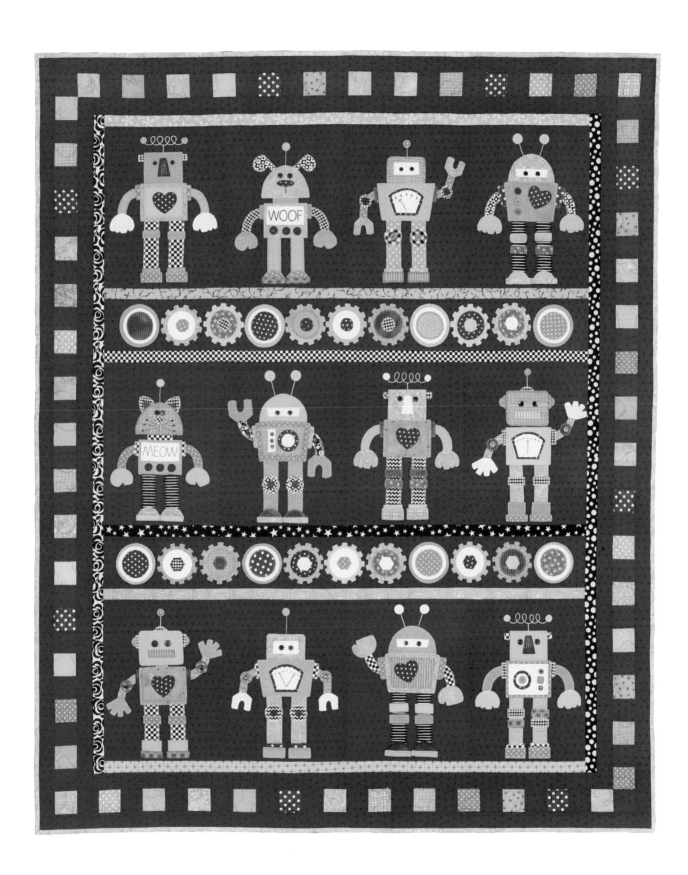

LITTLE ROBOT
SOFT TOY

Finished Size: 18" (45.7cm) tall

Materials

1 fat quarter (45.7cm × 55.9cm) of bright red wool felt for the head and body

1 fat eighth (45.7cm × 27.9cm) of gray wool felt for the arms and legs

8" (20.3cm) square of bright orange wool felt for the shoes, body and face appliqué

8" (20.3cm) square of bright purple wool felt for the shoes and body appliqué

8" × 13" (20.3cm × 33cm) rectangle of bright yellow wool felt for the claws, body appliqué and antenna

5" × 6" (12.7cm × 15.2cm) rectangle of bright jade green wool felt for the face appliqué

8" (20.3cm) square of bright pink wool felt for the claws

6" (15.2cm) square of white wool felt for the body and face appliqué

Scraps of magenta and lime green wool felt for the body appliqué

6" × 3" (15.2cm × 7.6cm) rectangle of bright blue wool felt for the antenna stalk and body appliqué

2" × 3" (5.1cm × 7.6cm) rectangle of bright green wool felt for the ears

Assorted Supplies

Light lead pencil

Fabric marking pen

Black embroidery floss for the facial features

Matching thread to suit your favorite method of appliqué

Temporary fabric basting glue (I used Roxanne's Temporary Basting Glue)

2 small black buttons for the eyes

5 tiny black buttons for the dial

Polyester fiberfill

Tracing paper (optional)

5 *Little Robot Soft Toy* template pages

Cutting Instructions

Trace and cut out the template pieces. You will need to trace the head, front body, back body, arm, claw, leg, shoe and antenna square pieces. Pin the template pieces to the fabrics you have chosen and cut the following:

Red Felt

Cut 2 head pieces (cut 1 in reverse).

Cut 1 front body piece.

Cut 2 back body pieces (cut 1 in reverse).

Blue Felt

Cut (2) ¾" × 3" (1.9cm × 7.6cm) rectangles for the antenna stalk.

Green Felt

Cut (4) ¾" × 1¼" (1.9cm × 3.2cm) rectangles for the ears.

Gray Felt

Cut 4 arm pieces (cut 2 in reverse).

Cut 4 leg pieces (cut 2 in reverse).

Yellow Felt

Cut 2 claw pieces (cut 1 in reverse).

Cut 2 antenna squares.

Pink Felt

Cut 2 claw pieces (cut 1 in reverse).

Orange Felt

Cut 2 shoe pieces (cut 1 in reverse).

Purple Felt

Cut 2 shoe pieces (cut 1 in reverse).

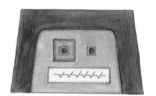

Figure 1: Head

Figure 2: Front Body Shape

Figure 3: Back Head Shape

Make the Robot

Note: A short 1.5 stitch length and a ¼" (6mm) seam are used throughout.

1. Trace the required face and body appliqué pieces from the template pages onto the paper side of the fusible webbing using a sharp pencil; leave ½" (1.3cm) between each piece. Cut the pieces out roughly, leaving ¼" (6mm) of paper around each pieces.

   You will need to cut 7 squares, 1 triangle, 1 mouth, 1 dial, 1 body panel and 1 face.

2. Fuse the pieces to the felt you have chosen following the manufacturer's instructions. Cut the pieces out carefully on the lines when cool. Remove the backing paper from the appliqué pieces and use the templates as a guide to fuse them to the front and back head pieces and the front body pieces.

3. Stitch around the appliqué pieces using your favorite method. (I used hand-stitched blanket stitch and 2 strands of matching embroidery floss.) Sew 2 black buttons to the face for eyes and 5 tiny black buttons

to the dial using strong thread (Figures 1, 2 and 3). Knot securely. Draw the mouth on the robot and backstitch using 2 strands of black embroidery floss.

4. Pin and then sew the front head piece to the front body piece with right sides facing (Figure 4). Set it aside. Press the seam open.

5. Use a small amount of basting glue to baste the ears and antenna stalks together in matching pairs. Blanket-stitch around the edges of each ear and the antenna stalk to sew the 2 layers together. Use 2 strands of matching embroidery floss and sew through both thicknesses of felt. Set the ears aside.

6. Place the finished antenna stalk between the 2 antenna squares and use a dot of basting glue to hold them in place. Using blanket stitch and 2 strands of embroidery floss, start stitching close to the antenna stalk on 1 side and work around the square, sewing through 2 thicknesses of felt, until you reach the opposite side of the stalk.

Continue to blanket-stitch the remainder of the square, sewing through 1 side only, to secure it to the antenna stalk. Knot the thread to secure, then flip the antenna over and repeat to stitch the opposite side of the square to the stalk. Knot the thread and bury the tail in the felt.

7. Use the template as a guide to position the ears and antenna right sides down and facing inward on the front head piece. Leave approximately 1" (2.5cm) overhang on the antenna. Pin and then baste them to the body (Figure 5). Set aside.

8. Sew the 2 back body pieces together with right sides facing. Leave the seam open where marked on the template. Press the seam open. Pin and then sew the back head piece to the joined back body pieces with right sides facing (Figure 6). Press the seam open.

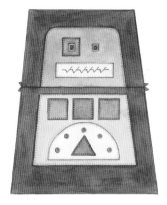

Figure 4

Figure 5

Figure 6

NEAT STITCHES

When you are blanket-stitching the felt shapes together, make sure the needle passes through the two layers of felt at a 90-degree angle. This ensures a neat stitch on both sides of the shape.

Figure 7

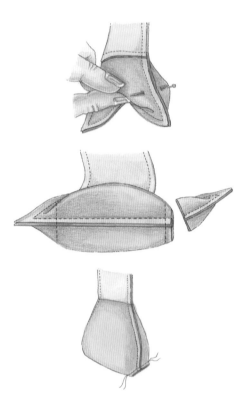

Figure 8

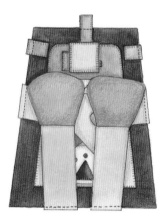

Figure 9

9. Sew a claw to the bottom of each arm with right sides facing. Pin and then sew the arms together in pairs with right sides facing. Leave the top and side seams open where marked on the template (Figure 7). Carefully notch the seams and turn the arms right-side out through the top opening.

10. Sew the shoes to the legs, then sew the legs together in the same way. Notch the seams as before, but do not turn the legs right sides out.

11. Fold 1 bottom corner of the shoe so the side and bottom seams are centered on top of each other. Pin. Stitch across the triangle formed by this fold, sewing approximately ⅜" (1cm) in from the pointy edge. Sew across the seam twice to strengthen the base.

    Repeat to sew the opposite bottom corner. Trim the corners approximately ¼" (6mm) from the stitching line (Figure 8). Turn the leg right-side out. Repeat for the second shoe shape.

12. Place the front of the robot right-side up on your work surface. Use the template as a guide to position the arms and legs right sides down and facing inward on the body. Make sure the stuffing openings are facing downward on the arms and inward on the legs. Pin and then baste them to the robot (Figure 9). The arms and legs are not stuffed until the robot is completed.

13. Place the front of the robot right-side up on your work surface again. Fold the antenna, ears, arms and legs in toward the center of the body. Place the back of the robot on top of the front of the robot, right sides facing. Pin the shapes together well to secure. Sew around the robot using a short stitch length, being careful to catch only the basted ends of the arms, legs, antenna and ears in the seams (Figure 10). Backstitch at the beginning and end of each seam.

14. Fold 1 bottom corner of the body so the side and bottom seams are centered on top of each other. Pin. Stitch across the triangle formed by this fold, sewing approximately ¾" (1.9cm) in from the pointy edge. Stitch across this seam twice to strengthen the base. Repeat to sew the opposite bottom corner. Trim the corners approximately ⅜" (1cm) from the stitching line (Figure 11).

15. Gently turn the robot right-side out through the back opening and stuff the body, arms and legs until firm. Hand-stitch the openings closed.

Figure 10

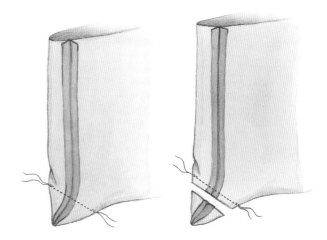

Figure 11

INDEX

www.fwcommunity.com

20   19   18   17   16   5   4   3   2   1

Distributed in Canada by Fraser Direct
100 Armstrong Avenue
Georgetown, ON, Canada L7G 5S4
Tel: (905) 877-4411

Distributed in the U.K. and Europe by F&W MEDIA INTERNATIONAL
Brunel House, Newton Abbot, Devon, TQ12 4PU, England
Tel: (+44) 1626 323200, Fax: (+44) 1626 323319
E-mail: enquiries@fwmedia.com

Distributed in Australia by Capricorn Link
P.O. Box 704, S. Windsor NSW, 2756 Australia
Tel: (02) 4560 1600, Fax: (02) 4577 5288
E-mail: books@capricornlink.com.au

SRN: T7179
ISBN-13: 978-1-4402-4447-6

Edited by Stephanie White
Designed by Nicola DosSantos
Production coordinated Jennifer Bass
Photography by Frank Rivera and Stephanie Hannus
Illustrations by Angela Atherton

METRIC CONVERSION CHART

To convert	to	multiply by
Inches	Centimeters	2.54
Centimeters	Inches	0.4
Feet	Centimeters	30.5
Centimeters	Feet	0.03
Yards	Meters	0.9
Meters	Yards	1.1

DEDICATION

This book is dedicated to lovers of fabric, color, coffee and cake, and to those of you who take little pieces of fabric and turn them into glorious quilts. May you be happy always! xx

ACKNOWLEDGMENTS

Writing this book has been a real journey, a culmination of dreams, which wouldn't have been possible without the help and support of some amazing people.

My first thanks go to my wonderfully creative family. Heartfelt thanks to my husband, Martin, and my three children, Kate, Chris and Kelly, who have supported me through every step of this creative journey. They have put up with odd meals, threads in and on every possession and fabric draped over every surface. They have hugged me when needed, ensured my coffee cup was never empty and coaxed me across the finish line. I love you.

Thanks also to my grandmother, Maude, who instilled the love of fabric in me and encouraged me every step of the way in my early years. You were the one who gave me my first needle and thread and let me string your buttons into long, glittering ropes. I miss you so much and wish you were here to see this book being published.

Huge thanks to the people at F+W who gave me the opportunity to do this. To Amelia Johanson for liking my work enough to ask me to do a book, and to Stephanie White for being such a wonderfully patient editor.

Many, many thanks to Fiona Robinson, an amazing quilter who brilliantly transformed flimsy tops into gorgeous quilts. I couldn't have done this without you. I hope I haven't worn you out; coffee and cake is on me. Bear hugs to Kris Meares for keeping me on track; for the endless texts, phone calls and emails telling me I could do this; and for the encouragement I needed to keep going when my deadlines seemed impossible to meet.

Last, but certainly not least, thank you to the lovely people on the Internet, most of whom I've never met, who have sent messages of love and encouragement. It is for you that this book is named, the title taken from the many emails you have sent telling me that my quilts make you happy and smile. This book is for you. Thank you for everything, toni xx

ABOUT THE AUTHOR

I live in Brisbane, Australia, with my husband, three grown children, two mischievous ginger kitties, a tribe of dust bunnies and a wall-to-wall fabric collection.

I have been sewing on and off for most of my life. My grandmother was a professional dressmaker, and my earliest memory is of playing with her button collection. She made the most amazing clothes for my Barbie dolls, perfect little re-creations of the dresses she was making in real life for her clients. I would traipse along with her to the local fabric stores, marveling at the wonderful fabrics, towering bolts of glorious color and texture. She encouraged me and never laughed at my childish efforts.

We moved away from my grandmother's home town when I was 12, and for a while I didn't sew anymore—apart from a memorable life-sized human doll for an art assignment in high school! It wasn't until the birth of my first daughter that I began to sew again. I rediscovered my love of fabric when I had to make clothes for a toddler who was too tiny for commercially sized clothing.

The quilting industry was small in Australia at this time. Quilting fabric was hard to get, and the colors were very limited. I was itching to try my hand at making a quilt, but everything was so uninspiring. As the quilting movement gained momentum, more and more fabric made its way into Australia—brighter fabrics, more choices. I was ready to make my first quilt, a simple creation made from soft brushed cotton in the palest yellows. We still have that quilt, draped over the lounge: no longer yellow, no longer pristine, but still loved twenty years later.

I soon discovered I couldn't follow a quilt pattern without wanting to rearrange the blocks and make the quilt more personal to me. I drove a lot of teachers to distraction! Then a friend I met through an online quilt group asked me to do some sewing for her quilt shop. She opened up the world of design and fabric to me. Carey introduced me to Catherine Sanchez, the then editor of Australian *Homespun* magazine, and got me my first magazine commission. Her shop no longer exists, but I will always be grateful to Carey and to the quilt group for their encouragement and support during those tentative beginnings.

I find myself now very far from those humble beginnings. I have done so many magazine projects that I've lost count, and I've sewn hundreds of quilts. My love of color, fabric and design is still as strong as it was when I first discovered it at my grandmother's side. I blog at www.theredbootquiltcompany.com as often as I can find the time, so please come on over and say hi.

MAKE YOURSELF HAPPY WITH MORE GREAT BOOKS!

Sew Fun: 20 Projects for the Whole Family

by Deborah Fisher

ISBN: 978-1-5966-8760-8

$26.99

Deborah Fisher has developed a range of projects that will appeal to adults and children alike. Fun costumes, beautiful dolls, story-time blankets, and communal quilts are just some of the projects included here. Enjoy combining bright colors and contemporary fabrics while spending time with the family. Get tips for working with children and learn how to involve them in ways that are enjoyable and stress-free.

The Quilter's Appliqué Workshop: Timeless Techniques for Modern Designs

by Kevin Kosbab

ISBN: 978-1-5966-8861-2

$26.99

A fresh take on quilting and appliqué! Kevin Kosbab shows quilters that not only is appliqué fun and easy to do, it can open up a world of design possibilities. *The Quilter's Appliqué Workshop* teaches quilters everything they need to know to create appliqué—both as embellishment and as the focus of projects. The book is divided into three sections that each explore a basic appliqué approach: raw-edge, prepared-edge, and needle-turn appliqué.